Benjamin Hall Kennedy

Occasional Sermons Preached Before the University of Cambridge

and...

Benjamin Hall Kennedy

Occasional Sermons Preached Before the University of Cambridge and...

ISBN/EAN: 9783744782340

Printed in Europe, USA, Canada, Australia, Japan

Cover: Foto ©Lupo / pixelio.de

More available books at **www.hansebooks.com**

OCCASIONAL SERMONS

PREACHED BEFORE THE

UNIVERSITY OF CAMBRIDGE

AND ELSEWHERE,

WITH AN

APPENDIX OF HYMNS.

BY

BENJAMIN HALL KENNEDY, D.D.,

REGIUS PROFESSOR OF GREEK, CAMBRIDGE, AND CANON OF ELY.

London:
GEORGE BELL AND SONS.
CAMBRIDGE: DEIGHTON, BELL AND CO.
1877

TO HIS GRACE

WILLIAM DUKE OF DEVONSHIRE, K.G.,

CHANCELLOR OF THE UNIVERSITY OF CAMBRIDGE,

THIS VOLUME IS INSCRIBED

WITH THE GRATITUDE FELT BY THE WRITER

AND THE RESPECT FELT BY ALL.

CONTENTS.

SERMON I.
The Magian Visit 1

SERMON II.
The Moral Excellence of Jesus 15

SERMON III.
Jesus the King of his People 33

SERMON IV.
The Interpretation of the Bible 49

SERMON V.
Sinful Party-Spirit exemplified in the Jewish Sanhedrim 68

SERMON VI.
The Fear of the World exemplified in Pontius Pilate 82

SERMON VII.
Socialism and Christianity 98

SERMON VIII.
The Balance of Duties in Education . . 113

SERMON IX.
The Departure of the Aged Christian . . 133

SERMON X.
ORDINATION 145

SERMON XI.
THE DOCTRINE OF THE HOLY TRINITY . . . 155

SERMON XII.
CHRISTIAN MISSIONS 167

SERMON XIII.
THE SAFEGUARDS OF CHRISTIAN BOYHOOD . . . 178

SERMON XIV.
THE COMMEMORATION OF BENEFACTORS . . . 189

SERMON XV.
ON THE DEATH OF THE PRINCE CONSORT . . . 204

SERMON XVI.
PAPAL SUPREMACY 215

ON THE JUDGMENT IN THE GORHAM CASE . . 223

SERMON XVII.
THE CHRIST OF PROPHECY 231

APPENDIX.
PSALMS AND HYMNS 247

APPENDIX TO SERMONS 288

SERMON I.

THE MAGIAN VISIT.

BEFORE THE UNIVERSITY OF CAMBRIDGE, JAN. 6, 1861.

ST LUKE II. 32.

A Light to lighten the Gentiles.

AMONG the titles given by the early Church to the Feast we this day celebrate, two are more especially prominent: —Theophany, or manifestation of God; and Epiphany, dawn of light, or, sudden appearance. Both titles are well adapted to every Manifestation of our Lord and Saviour Jesus Christ. For God was in Christ, reconciling the world unto Himself. Christ is called Emmanuel, God with us; and in Him dwelleth all the fulness of the Godhead bodily. Again: Christ was foretold as the Sun of Righteousness, who should arise with healing in his wings. He reveals Himself as the bright and morning star. He is declared by his own beloved Apostle to be the Light of men. Once more: Christ appeared indeed in the fulness of the time determined and foretold : yet was He born suddenly into the world which was made by Him and knew Him not. Angel visits and dreams were required to prepare a few chosen persons for Messiah's birth. Angel songs drew a few poor shepherds, firstfruits and types of Jewish faith, to the manger in the city of David, where Christ the Lord was cradled, a new-born babe. Suddenly, as Malachi had said aforetime, did the Lord come to his temple on the day of his Presentation : and none knew Him save one aged Rabbi, just and devout, waiting for the consolation of Israel, and one widow of about fourscore and four years, who served God with fastings and prayers night and day. The former of these holy persons, Simeon, came by the Spirit into the temple, and took up the child Jesus in his arms, and blessed God, and said, 'Lord, now lettest Thou thy servant depart in peace, according to thy word: for mine eyes have seen thy salvation, which Thou hast prepared before the face of all people : a Light to lighten the Gentiles, and the glory of thy people Israel.' But not to these circumstances only, nor to these chiefly, did the early Church apply the term Epiphany. It was applied principally to the Baptism of Jesus in the river Jordan, when the dove-like Spirit and the heavenly Voice manifested Him to all the people there assembled, as the beloved Son, in whom the Father was well pleased. It was applied also to the beginning of miracles which Jesus did in Cana of Galilee, whereby 'He manifested forth his glory, and the disciples believed on Him.' But when, in the fourth century, the Nativity of our Lord had been determined to the 25th day of December, twelve following days were in process of time set apart for the festivities of Christmas, ending with the Feast of the Epiphany on this day, which has since been held in the Church to commemorate the Manifestation of Christ to the Gentiles, that is, to the Wise-men, or Magians, who came from the East to worship the new-born King of the Jews. Thus we have two Epiphanies of the infant Saviour, one to the Jews, the shepherds of Bethlehem, the other to the Gentiles, the Eastern Magians: and two Epiphanies of the adult Saviour, when He began his prophetic work: one, in his Baptism, to the Jews, the other, in his first Miracle, to his disciples. It has indeed been well said that every one of his miracles was an Epiphany: and if we look beyond the time when, having wrought the work of redemption on earth, He was received up into glory, we find two Epiphanies of the Lord to Paul and Peter, whereby it was made manifest that the partition-wall was now thrown down, and the Church of Christ opened to Gentile as well as Jew. And are not all who name his Name sincerely, looking for a final Epiphany, even that blessed hope and the glorious appearing of the great God and our Saviour Jesus Christ? O my brethren, how can that glorious appearing be a blessed hope to any of the sinful children of men, unless they have received into their own hearts, through faith, the spiritual Epiphany of that true Light, which alone gives us power to become the sons of God?

The subject matter of the present Festival—the journey of the Magians, as recorded in the Gospel for the day—opens a large field for thought and enquiry. May it be blest to our edification.

Vague tradition, resting, it would seem, on no stronger basis than the threefold offering of gold, frankincense, and myrrh, has pronounced these Magians to be three in number: and the same tradition, finding in their pilgrimage the fulfilment of those old predictions, that the kings of Arabia and Saba should bring gifts, and that kings should come to the brightness of Messiah's rising, has exalted them to the rank of emirs or petty kings. We know how large a place they hold in mediæval legend : how often Christian Art has clothed them with the forms and colours of painting : how Christian Architecture has enshrined them in one of its most splendid works, the Choir at Cologne. But in the sterner divinity of the Reformed Church, which interprets Scripture chiefly by its own light, admitting tradition only as corroborative evidence, and that with great caution, the number of the Magian visitors remains undefined, and it is left an open question, whether, from their title, we conclude them to have been astrologers from Chaldea, or priests of the Mazdean faith from Persia.

Difficulties there are belonging to this Magian visit and its immediate results (as stated in the 2nd Chapter of St Matthew), the flight into Egypt, the murder of the Infants, the return of the holy Family, and their settlement at Nazareth: difficulties perhaps more numerous and various than are found in any scriptural passage of the same length. The source to which the Magians seem to ascribe their information—'we have seen his star in the East';—the star itself, and the motions assigned to it; the perplexing order of events in St Matthew as compared with those of the same period in St Luke's Gospel; the silence of Josephus respecting the massacre of the Infants: the questions raised by the citations from the Old Testament which are said to be fulfilled: these are the principal objections arrayed against the Gospel narrative by the atheist, the pantheist, the deist, and the rationalist, who, differ as they may on other points, agree in discrediting the supernatural facts of Scripture, and in denying its supreme authority as an inspired book. But the thoughtful Christian is dismayed by no difficulties in Holy Writ, which do not involve a contradiction of some recognized truth. Such as merely imply that a question is dark or doubtful, because some knowledge requisite for its elucidation is withheld from us, may employ his mind, but they cannot distress it. He regards these difficulties as occasions for the exercise of humility and faith; and he is well content to wait and pray till more light be given, or to remain ignorant, if it must be so, on this side the grave. Nay more: with Bishop Butler, he views the hard problems of the Bible as among the indications of its coming from Him who has given hard problems in the book of nature, to exercise the higher faculties of men, while what is really needful to life—to corporeal life in nature, to spiritual life in revelation—He has placed within the reach of all who desire to eat and be satisfied.

The cavils of a Strauss and a Bruno Bauer on this passage, and the answers they have received from Christian learning, we may leave, for the most part, to be more fitly considered in the study and the lecture-room than in the pulpit of God's house. But one objection there is, so nearly affecting the honour of God and our own edification, that we may not pursue our subject without some endeavour to remove it. St Matthew tells us that the Magians at Jerusalem spoke in this wise: 'Where is he that is born King of the Jews? for we have seen his star in the East, and are come to worship him.' Was then this star, whatever its precise nature, the real and sole medium through which God apprized them of Christ's birth? They might have had—we believe they had— previous expectation of such an event. But this does not get rid of the objection. Did the star alone make known the *fact?* If so, it could only be by virtue of some supposed principle of astrology. But judicial astrology, divination by means of the heavenly bodies, to a Christian mind implies nothing better than delusion or imposture. Can we for a moment suppose that God, the God of truth, He who hateth a lie, gave a true voice in this instance to astrology, and made its calculations to be tokens of his truth, yea, of his greatest truth, the central world-truth, the appearance of his Son in the flesh? We dare not think it. As reasonably, as reverently might we suppose that God would speak by the mouth of the Delphian priestess, and accredit her oracles. But if we refuse to believe this, do we then admit that the Magians spoke deceitfully, when they ascribed their knowledge to the star? that they, called and guided, as they must have been, by the grace of God, to be the first fruits of heathen faith in Christ, came to Jerusalem with a lie in their mouths? Once more, impossible. How then, it is further asked, do we untie the knot? We do not untie: we cut it. We say that this difficulty implies no more than that we do not know enough of the foregoing circumstances to explain how far the Magians meant to represent the sight of the star as their medium of information, and as the moving cause of their journey. That the birth of a mighty Jewish prince was looked for about this time in the East, is a well attested and acknowledged fact. That Daniel's great prediction was known to the learned of Persia and Chaldea, is not improbable. Jerusalem, its history, its politics and prospects, must have been deeply interesting to a people who had once held the Jews captive, among whom many Jews were still dispersed, and who regularly traded with Judea. The Magians then, we may well believe, were in a waiting frame of mind. It has been surmised (assuming that the Presentation in the Temple must certainly be dated some months before the Magians appeared at Jerusalem) that the reports of Simeon and Anna concerning Messiah's birth may have been conveyed to the East by some devout Jewish merchant. No such surmise is necessary. They may, as afterwards, have been warned and called of God in a dream, and waking to the sight of a new and bright star in the heavens, destined by God for their encouragement and guidance, they may, without any deceitful intention, have used those words at Jerusalem : 'We have seen'—or rather 'we saw his star in the East and came to worship him.' We put this solution as a bare possibility, without presuming to know more than God is pleased to tell us of the means by which He brings to bear his eternal purposes. Enough to have shown that our opponents fail to place the honour of God and the credit of his revelation on the horns of a moral dilemma.

The way should now be clear for a practical view of the subject before us.

And note: how bright a constellation of excellent virtues shines forth in the conduct of these Eastern pilgrims! In commencing the journey, what faith is theirs, what hope, what unhesitating obedience, what trust in God! In pursuing it, what perseverance and patience! At Jerusalem, what guilelessness yet what prudence, what reverent submission to God's written Word! When they draw near to Christ, what holy joy! In the house at Bethlehem, what humble devotion, what ample liberality, what readiness to pour forth the best of all they have for the service of their Saviour and their God! These great and truly Christian qualities shine with so clear a lustre in the story of these Magians, brief as it is, that we need not enlarge upon them severally, content with praying for grace to imitate as well as admire them.

But we would pause for a brief space, and observe the blessing which God gives to sincere faith, even when accompanied with imperfect knowledge. The Magians were called by the free grace of God: for 'no man,' saith our Lord, 'can come unto me, unless the Father, who hath sent me, draw him.' The warning of God and the sight of his star turned their eyes and their feet at once towards Jerusalem. Yet the new-born Infant, whom they went to worship, they knew not as the Son of God, as the Incarnate Word, who was in the beginning, and was with God, and was God, by whom the worlds were made. They knew him only as King of the Jews. Some great blessing they certainly hoped from Him, we know not exactly what: some victory, perhaps, of good over evil, some triumph of Ormuzd over Ahriman: or some universal reign of righteousness and peace. They believed with a vague faith, yet they obeyed with a clear and stedfast purpose. 'Lord, we believe,' was their virtual prayer, 'help Thou our unbelief.' And verily they were helped. Willing to do the will of the Father, they gained the knowledge of the true doctrine of his blessed Son. They were led from faith to faith; from faith in God's call and God's star during the journey, to faith in God's written Word at Jerusalem. They were led to higher and better things still; from faith to sight, from hope to fruition, from doubt and trial to assurance and joy. Travailing and heavy-laden they came to Jesus, and He, babe and suckling as He was, gave them rest. The enemy and avenger, the wily Herod, was baffled in his plots against them and against the Lord's Anointed. Being warned of God in a dream, the Magians departed into their own country another way. That way may have been longer and harder than the former: but now more than ever would the Lord be with them; his rod and his staff would comfort them: surely goodness and mercy followed them all the days of their life, and they dwell in the house of the Lord for ever. May we meet them there in the resurrection of the just.

But if we are to stand with the Magians in the congregation of the righteous hereafter, ours too must be a faith like theirs.in this our earthly pilgrimage: a faith that can turn its back on all things else to seek and find Christ: a faith that can overcome the world, and avoid the snares it lays to entrap the feet of those who are bound to a better country: a faith that can look on pomps and vanities with indifference, or rather with pity, and discern the great and the good, the beautiful and the divine, in things which to unpurged eyes are least and poorest: a faith which values human lore only so far as it points to Christ and may be made the means of showing Him to the world; which prizes human wealth only so far as it can be used to extend the kingdom of God, and make his creatures happier and better: a faith which prays ever to be sustained and increased by the power of the Holy Spirit in the heart, yet ever looks abroad for occasions of strengthening itself by action for God's honour and the good of men: a humble, a thankful, a hopeful, a self-denying faith, a faith that works by love; in short, the justifying faith of Scripture. If this faith be ours, then, in the season now ended, we shall have shared the Christmas gladness of the Jewish Shepherds, praising and glorifying God for the birth of Him, through whom we, personally, have peace with God. The New Year will have found us looking behind and before us with Christian eyes, humbled and penitent for past sins, grateful for mercies received, rejoicing in hope, patient in tribulation, resolved, through the grace of God, to work with and for our divine Master in this present year, watching unto prayer, that if we be called to Him, or He come to us, in the course of it, we may be found ready. The Day of our Lord's Circumcision, foreshadowing Good Friday, will have taught us its proper lessons; that we have a Saviour, a Jesus, who, sinless Himself, lived and died to save us, not *in* our sins, but *from* our sins; that we serve One whose example binds us to fulfil all righteousness, and to deny worldly lusts; for that we must through much tribulation enter into the kingdom of God. And so should we now be fit to keep the Festival of this day in the sense which the Church gives to it, as the Manifestation of Christ to the Gentiles, as the great Mission-feast of the Church.

When holy Simeon spoke the words of my text, there was no veil upon his heart, as upon the hearts of other Jews. The whole stream of prophetic light flowed in rich abundance through his inspired soul. He read aright the promise of God to Abraham and Isaac, that in their seed all the nations of the earth should be blessed. He saw the dawning of the day, when Ishmael should come home again, and Esau be hated no more. The dark speech uttered upon David's harp was not dark to him. He knew to whom the heathen should be given for an inheritance, and the uttermost parts of the earth for a possession. That dim prediction of Zion's future glories, the eighty-seventh Psalm, he could read by the clearer splendours which later prophecy sheds from the sixtieth and following chapters of the Book of Isaiah: 'Arise, shine, for thy light is come, and the glory of the Lord is risen upon thee.' And he would remember that, when the prophetic spirit of Israel breathed its last on the lips of Malachi, the Lord thus spake through his latest interpreter: 'From the rising of the sun even to the going down of the same my Name shall be great among the Gentiles, and in every place incense shall be offered unto my Name, and a peace-offering.'

Of these prophecies, my brethren, are not we ourselves a living fulfilment, we, sprung from heathen ancestors, in a once heathen land? Upon us hath not the true light shined, even the Gospel of Jesus Christ, the Son of God, the Saviour of the world? Have we not all been received by Him in holy baptism? Has He not, by his ministers, taken us into his arms, and signed us with the sign of his cross and blessed us, and given to us power to become the sons of God, even to them that believe on his Name? When we have wandered from Him, the true Shepherd, has not his loving voice restored us, and led us in the paths of righteousness? And, when we return to Him with sighs and tears of repentance, does He not forgive our sins, and prepare a table for us in the wilderness of this world, and feed us with the cup of salvation and the bread of life? 'O that men would therefore praise the Lord for his goodness, and declare the wonders that He doeth for the children of men!'

Or when we lift up our eyes to the world around us, through the gross darkness which covers large populations of the earth see we not light after light flashing up, and in many a moral desert a pathway made for Him, who is alone the way, the truth, and the life to all mankind? And although that East, from which the

Magians travelled to adore the Infant Light, is now the darkest home of heathendom, although many a generation may pass, ere He, to whom a thousand years are as one day, shall make the false stars of Buddha and Brahma and Mohammed to vanish from the human horizon, yet year by year their light pales before the advancing beams of the Sun of righteousness. Meanwhile Ethiopia stretches out her hands unto God: on every Atlantic coast the mariner hears the sound of Sabbath bells: over the breadth of the vast Pacific—well-omened name—the Lord reigneth, let the earth rejoice; yea, the multitude of the isles may be glad thereof. 'O that men would therefore praise the Lord for his goodness, and declare the wonders that He doeth for the children of men!'

Enough is here to rejoice in: yet our joy should be mingled with fear. Let us look well to our own candlestick, that it be not removed from its place. Let us tremble lest the light, which is lightening the Gentiles in other lands, be burning but too dimly in our own. Within these British Isles, nominally Christian, there is enough of virtual heathenism to employ all the missionaries of all Christendom: heathenism of many a Lazarus whom the Church cannot reach, heathenism, alas, of many a Dives, who will not hear the Church. And all this time,—O shame and sorrow!—Christians—yea, Christian Churchmen—are at war among themselves, when they should be standing side by side against their common foes, vice and ignorance and infidelity. May the time past suffice to have wrought such madness! May we, each and all, pray and strive for more Christian love, Christian brotherhood, Christian zeal! Yes, may each strive in love, that all may strive in union! Society is but an aggregate of individuals : and all individuals have the same moral and religious wants. The faith which can change your heart and mine, has the power to transform society itself. The truth which sanctifies the man, sanctifies human nature. The light which illuminates one soul, dispels the moral darkness of the world. O Christians in name, be Christians in deed and in truth, in heart and in life. All things are possible to him that believeth. The Light that now lightens the Gentiles from Oregon to China shone first in a stable at Bethlehem and in a carpenter's shop at Nazareth. Received in the power of faith by a few lowly and despised Galileans, it became the vital principle of human civilization. Let us walk as children of *that* light: so shall we realize our Lord's promise, and like Himself, like his Apostles, we too in our sphere and in our degree shall be the light of the world. 'For Zion's sake we shall not hold our peace, and for Jerusalem's sake we shall not rest, until the righteousness thereof go forth as brightness, and the salvation thereof as a lamp that burneth.'

SERMON II.

THE MORAL EXCELLENCE OF JESUS.

BEFORE THE UNIVERSITY OF CAMBRIDGE, JAN. 13, 1861.

St John xiv. 1.

Ye believe in God; believe also in Me.

'No man hath seen God at any time,' says the Evangelist St John in his first chapter: and so far religion and irreligion hold the same language.

'No man hath seen God at any time,' says the Materialist: therefore, for aught we know, the things which are seen may have existed for ever, and may go on to exist for ever, in form manifold and mutable, but in substance always the same.

'No man hath seen God at any time,' says the Pantheist: for God is the One in All, and the All in One, absolute, infinite, incomprehensible; and things which are seen, whether we call them good or evil, yea, we ourselves, are but so many phases of the one divine essence, bubbles, as it were, that rise and float for awhile on the ocean of Godhead, and then sink into its bosom for ever.

'No man hath seen God at any time,' says the philosophic Theist: but I believe in a personal God; and, if you ask me for the arguments on which I rest my belief, I reply: They are many and various, some drawn from my own consciousness, others from outward experience. If you further ask: Do any or all of these arguments amount to a demonstration of the existence of God? I reply: No; for demonstration implies definition, and the Infinite defined is a contradiction in terms: demonstration involves the assumption of a first principle; but God Himself is prior to any principle, and therefore, by the nature of the case, indemonstrable. Believing that I have in my own consciousness, as guiding instincts, the ideas of existence, of freedom, and of duty or morality, I further believe that I have the idea of the perfection of each of these ideas, that is, the idea of the Absolute and Infinite, that is, the idea of God. This idea of perfection is necessarily vague and incomplete, because my nature is relative and finite, and the relative has no measure for the absolute, nor the finite for the infinite. But as I believe in a perfectly moral Being, on whom all things depend, I must believe that all things are directed to serve a perfectly moral purpose. I do then believe that this idea of perfection is given for the purpose of lifting my eyes to the distant hills, behind which absolute Truth hides its awful beauty; for the purpose of pricking me on towards that far distant but ever desired and alone desirable goal: for the purpose of raising me ever higher and higher in the scale of being, of drawing me ever nearer and nearer to God. Furthermore, from that restless quest of the Better which I find inherent in my nature, from my thirsting desire of intimate and abiding communion with the true and the beautiful, as also from comparing the notions of justice and love, which are implied in the divine perfection, with the wrongs and inequalities and sufferings of human life, I am irresistibly led to believe in the immortal existence of man, and in a future state of retribution.

'No man hath seen God at any time,' says the Christian; this is an admitted, and to me a revealed, truth. I accept and approve all that has been said by the philosophic Theist; but I cannot rest where he rests. I feel a strong and ardent desire to know more of the true and living God, more of my relations with Him, more of my duties to Him, more of my hopes from Him, than reason and experience are able to teach me. As He has given me this desire, and as the things desired are good in themselves, I may hope that He, the All-just and All-wise, will in some just and wise manner and measure deign to satisfy it. I may pray for a divine revelation of things divine; and the more so as I find that the profoundest and purest of heathen philosophers, a Socrates and a Plato, acknowledged the same desire, and authorized the same prayer. But there is yet a keener thought goading me on, and allowing me no rest. I owe to God duties, which I never have fully paid, which I never can fully pay. I find in myself, and see everywhere around me, not only pain and sorrow, but also moral evil, rooted in human nature, bearing poisonous fruit, and propagating itself in all directions. O God, what remedy? what dare I hope from thy justice, which I have violated, from thy love, which I have slighted? I want the hope of pardon and reconciliation with God. I want help from Him to fight against the power of evil in and around me. I want to see my brother-men helped to fight the same battle. I want to be assured that I shall not carry this evil with me beyond the grave, that it will not pursue me and my brothers into our future state, and cleave to us there, an incurable leprosy, for ever. This it is that forbids me to be satisfied with the natural religion of the philosophic Theist. This it is that drives me to prayer. This obliges me to cry with an exceeding bitter cry: O my Father, who hast deigned to make me as I am, and to give me the desire of being with Thee for ever, deign also to be my Saviour from the evil, and my Guide unto Thyself, who art the fountain of all good. And I believe that this cry, the cry of suffering humanity, has been heard. Nay, rather I believe that it was anticipated in God's everlasting purpose. I do not pretend to explain creation. I do not pretend to explain the existence of evil. They are beyond the reach of my finite understanding. But I know they do exist: and I find in books claiming to speak in God's name an account of God's dispensations in regard to them, which, taken as a whole, meets and satisfies the cravings of my spirit. I see the world created, and man in the image of God, pure and happy, but free. I see man tempted, and yielding to temptation; sin entering into the world, and death by sin. But, as soon as the disease breaks out, I see the remedy proclaimed, even the restoration of man to the favour of God and to the capacity of holiness, by means of a Redeemer, the seed of the woman, to be born in the fulness of time. I see a peculiar people, a peculiar ritual, a peculiar history, arranged and directed by God to prepare those great events of redemption, the birth, life, death and resurrection of this Saviour. At the same time I observe the traditions of heathen mythology teeming with hints of this great story, and the currents of profane history converging towards a central point and a great world-era. The hour at length strikes: the Word is made flesh, and dwells among men; and, although no man hath seen God at any time, the only-begotten Son, who is in the bosom of the Father, He hath revealed Him. And not only does He reveal God, not only does He bring life and immortality to light, but He willingly underwent death and the grave, to take away the sins of the world, that all who believe in Him might not perish, but have everlasting life. Finally, having risen again, and having been received up into glory, He sent forth his Holy Spirit to comfort his followers, and bear witness with their spirits that they are the sons of God. Therefore am I a Christian. Therefore, when my Saviour says to his disciples in the words of the text, 'Ye believe in God, believe also in Me,' I hasten to reply with humble rapture : 'Lord, I believe ; help Thou mine unbelief.'

Why the believer in God should also believe in Christ appears from the words, already cited, of St John, that He who revealed God to men is the only-begotten Son, who is in the bosom of the Father; words figuratively denoting the intimate and essential union of Christ and God. The same doctrine is taught by Jesus Himself, in the passage which nearly follows my text: 'he that hath seen me hath seen the Father': and elsewhere, 'I and the Father are One.'

Such being the claims advanced by Jesus to a participation in the divine nature, and so exalted the character of his doctrine, are we not entitled, nay, morally compelled, to expect a corresponding character in his human life, in all that He did, and all that He was, here on earth? For He, whose thoughts and lessons and commandments were those of God, must, by strict consequence, have lived a divine life, even while dwelling as a man with men. He who in his ethical system set before mankind a standard of holiness, must have realized this ideal in Himself, must Himself have been holy in all his walk and conversation. And the facts do indeed answer so truly to this expectation, that the transcendant moral excellence of Jesus has from the first been used as an argument for his divine mission. Nay, we find that He himself appeals to this proof. And a proof it is not less obvious than forcible. For the earthly life of Jesus is the very counterpart and fulfilment of his doctrine. It displays a pattern of holiness, such as human history cannot parallel, such as cannot be explained by any human attributes, but only by the supposition of a divine nature dwelling and working in Him. This proof has the further advantage of being both generally intelligible and powerfully convincing, since it exhibits the thing which is to be proved not in abstract notions, but in a living reality, plainly showing that no excellence of heart or mind, no human virtue, can be named, of which we do not find in Christ the most perfect type and example. And those types and examples extend to every state and relation of human life; since the Son of Man, that He might be the perfect pattern of humanity, was in all points tempted like as we are, yet without sin.

The evangelical narratives, which acquaint us with the life of Jesus, are the more trustworthy, as they are evidently not written for the express purpose of drawing a portrait of moral perfection, or executing an elaborate panegyric. With artless simplicity, and in few words, the writers produce the acts and sayings of Jesus, usually without any comment of their own.

In this season of Epiphany, the Church directs our special attention to the active life of the Incarnate Son of God, as the great Prophet of the Church. Far be from us the vain and presumptuous thought of sounding that deep mystery of godliness, which angels desire to look into, the moral nature of Him who was very God and very Man. But, as none are Christians who do not abide in Him, and 'he that saith he abideth in Him ought himself also to walk even as He walked,' we may without presumption, if humbly and reverently and with inward prayer for the guidance of his Holy Spirit, review some of those features in the life and character of Jesus, which display Him first, as a model of human virtue, secondly, as something more than human, as, in that sense, divine.

As the first excellence in our Lord's human character, let us note his entire devotion to the will and work of the Father who sent Him. The Apostle to the Hebrews aptly puts in his mouth the prophetic words of his forefather David: 'I delight to do thy will, O my God.' And indeed our Lord so spake in his own person: 'My meat is to do the will of Him who sent me, and to finish his work.' To the will of the Father He had consecrated his earthly life, and accordingly that life became one series of uninterrupted exertion in the discharge of the task committed to Him, the redemption of fallen man. He went about, unwearied, from place to place, teaching men to know the one true God, and Jesus Christ whom He had sent. When the day had been spent in addressing and instructing men, the night was often given to prayer and communion with God. The same spirit of faithful devotion was shown in the resolute confidence which led Him to commence so vast an enterprise with means which seemed so slight and inadequate. Without name, without riches, without friends or followers, He appeared in public life. Soon afterwards, He had the pain of learning that his own townsmen, nay, his very relatives, had no faith in Him; that even honest and well-intentioned though erring men could say: 'Can any good come out of Nazareth?' But this dreary loneliness, this discouraging withdrawal of human support, had no power to shake the stedfast resolution of Him, who was urged by more than human motives to undertake God's work, and could therefore count on more than human support in achieving it. And so He still pursued the even tenour of his way, choosing his first disciples from the fishermen of the lake, and preaching his Gospel chiefly to the poor, though not refusing his advice and assistance, when sought by the rich and great.

If desertion had no power to discourage Jesus, neither did hindrance avail to restrain his activity. The leaders of the Jewish sects and schools, having more or less influence with the people, threw themselves in his way:—the scribes and teachers of the Law from envy, because He discarded their captious subtleties and unprofitable jargon, teaching as one, to whom authority was given from above:—the Pharisees from hatred and revenge, because He exposed their hypocrisy and ostentation, censured their immoral principles, and exacted a far nobler and truer holiness than theirs:—the Sadducees from contempt, because He did not, like them, recommend sensual enjoyment as the aim of human existence, but rather purity and holiness and endless life with God. Even the people, who expected a temporal Messiah, seeing no preparation made by Jesus to restore the throne of David, and hearing no exhortations from his mouth but those which called them to repentance, self-denial, purity, peace, and a kingdom of God in the heart, gradually forsook Him and his cause. Yet, in the face of all these impediments, so firm was his stedfastness, so calm his temper, so assured his trust, that in one of those trying seasons of desertion He offered to the few who still remained by his side the option of departing with the rest.

If the life and character of Jesus present the highest example of faithful devotion to the will and work of God, our admiration is also due to his principles and conduct in dealing with men. His tender love towards our race appears indeed from the facts already mentioned; for all his great achievements and sufferings were for the good of mankind. If the will of God was the motive, the salvation of man was the end. But, besides what He did and suffered for men, we have also to consider how He lived among them: we have to regard Him as a model of the social virtues. Though on every side He met with misunderstanding and contradiction, yet so constantly did He practise as well as teach peaceableness, forbearance, and forgiveness, that his best disciples were unable to comprehend and imitate Him. He, the strictest teacher of purity and truth, was yet so mild to the erring, so gentle to sinners, that his enemies imputed to Him laxity of principle. That loving compassion for the spiritual sicknesses of men, which moved Him to become their Redeemer and the Physician of their souls, was extended also to their bodily wants and ailments; and most of his great miracles were wrought to remove or palliate human suffering. From these good works He was diverted by no malice or ingratitude of wicked men. Slander and calumny were cast on Him, and his only reply was, to labour for the benefit of the slanderers and calumniators. Reviled and hated, He neither reviled nor hated in return: He repaid his enemies with love, and prayed for those who had nailed Him to the bitter cross. And although the great purpose of his mission reached to the whole human race, yet in every narrower circle of relative duty He was not the less a pattern of excellence. As a son, He remained in dutiful subjection to his human parents for a time much exceeding the usual years of tutelage: and almost his last words on the cross commended his mother to the care of his most beloved disciple. Christianity has sometimes, but unjustly, been reproached with omitting from its code of virtues friendship and patriotism. Yet the only tears which we know to have been shed by Jesus flowed beside the tomb of his friend Lazarus, and in view of the doomed metropolis of his native land. So loyally was He the friend of his countrymen, that to their welfare his public labours were almost wholly devoted: and, had they been capable of knowing the things which belonged to their peace, He would have saved them politically as well as morally.

But the grandeur of his character, in all that He undertook and carried on and achieved for the glory of God and the good of men, is not seen in its full light, until we take in the purity of his motives, his noble unselfishness, his high-minded indifference not to reward only, but even to recognition. The stimulants and attractions, which commonly prompt men to active exertion, He knew not, or, if He knew, heeded not. A man of sorrows, and acquainted with grief, often not having where to lay his head, He had bidden a long farewell to the enjoyments of earth and sense. Riches, the chief good of ordinary men, had no charm for Him. Honour and renown, the idols of a somewhat higher order of minds, were beneath his regard. Command and leadership, which so many seek and so few attain, and yet fewer rightly use, he put away from Him, and withdrew Himself from the multitude, when they were eager to march under his banner and proclaim Him their king. And why was this? even because the honour of his heavenly Father, the salvation of men, and the reign of truth and righteousness, were to Him all in all. These purposes, the best and the highest, occupied his entire soul. His single motive, the noblest and the purest, was to serve and advance these. For these alone He lived, and for these He died.

So far we have viewed the life and character of the man Christ Jesus as arriving at the summit of human perfection. Never man, we say, lived and spake as this man. Let us now, with reverent humility, consider those features in his character, which display to us a moral being superior to the highest human excellence, a being supernatural, and so what we deem divine: God stooping to the senses, and speaking to the heart of man.

And first, behold the sinlessness of our blessed Lord. This quality, though negative in form, has in this case a positive force, for, as it denies a property inherent in human nature, it marks the moral character of Jesus as a thing which transcends humanity, as invested with the purity which we ascribe to the divine essence. He was tempted as other men are tempted, yet He sinned not. He was tried, as few others have been tried, in every stage of his earthly calling, yet He sinned not. He had to bear the unteachableness of his disciples, the unstedfastness of his friends, the calumnies and persecution of his foes, the ingratitude of his nation, the treason of a trusted follower, the agonies of his closing life, the shame and torture of his cruel death; yet He sinned not. He endured all with a serenity of temper and a loftiness of soul, which after ages have regarded with admiring wonder, as placing Him above the nature of man, and attributable only to a divine element within Him. He could Himself venture to appeal to the testimony of his contemporaries, and before the face of his enemies He could say: 'Which of you convinceth me of sin?' And when those enemies had condemned Him to death for words of truth, which they represented as blasphemous, and demanded from the heathen ruler the confirmation of their sentence, the impartial verdict of that ruler declared: 'I find no fault in Him.'

Another and positive mark of superhuman excellence is the *equal* perfection of Jesus in *every* department of morals. Absolute holiness is indeed a thing we believe in without assuming that our imperfect faculties can actually comprehend it. But it is competent to us to form some judgment of that which indefinitely surpasses in greatness and goodness all our conceptions of our own powers, and all our experience of the powers of other men. And thus we say of the equal and universal holiness of our blessed Lord, that, human in kind (for, if not such, we could not estimate it at all), it is superhuman in degree. The finite individual mind rises in this life to relative perfection only, whether of knowledge or of virtue; and the very best minds have their own spheres of excellence; the best characters in history have their special vices or defects. But from whatever side we view the character of Jesus, in whatever direction we follow the tenour of his life and action, we everywhere find Him equally great, equally perfect. In his devotion to his calling, in his relations with God and with men, in social and public circles, in what He did and what He suffered, in struggle and in victory, in life and in death, from first to last, we have before us the same beautiful yet awful ideal, which every good man would fain reach, which every best man feels and owns his utter inability to approach.

A third feature, in which is seen the more than human excellence of our Lord's nature, is the moral equilibrium, which holds in just and harmonious proportion virtues seemingly contradictory to one another. The peculiarity of man's condition debars him from ever attaining this perfect equipoise. In reasoning (as notable instances at the present time remind us), he is continually baffled by the inability of his dialectic faculties to measure and define the vast conceptions of his inquiring mind. In his moral being, and in the conduct of life, he finds it so hard to reconcile conflicting duties, that, while in those, whom history ranks as great men, we often find the gravest faults, so is many a man of worth held back from greatness and even from usefulness by the very fear of going too far in this or that moral direction; and in corrupt times the popular ideal of excellence is the ability to make things easy and pleasant without allowing to moral and religious principle any power or right to become a disturbing force in the social system. In God alone, the absolute Being, free from all contradictions of the finite, moral virtues are combined in essential perfection and mutual harmony. Refracted and tinted in the world, in Him they shine with colourless and pure light. He is, in equable weight and measure, Lord and Father, just and merciful, chastening and forgiving, patient and prompt to interpose in due time. How strikingly does Christ exhibit Himself to us in this respect as the true Son of God, as indeed one with the Father! In His whole walk and conduct on earth we find this sublime union of the most opposite virtues; majesty with humility; zeal with gentleness; strength with tenderness; energy with composure; the wisdom and prudence of the sage with the simplicity of the dove and the candour of the child; all that is best and fairest in human nature raised and refined to all that can most be imagined of the divine.

Alas, in attempting to photograph, as it were, the character of the Saviour from the representation of inspired limners, how do our hands tremble, our lights err, our distances deceive, our results fall short of the perfect loveliness of the great original : so that what is said of the King of kings and Lord of lords, we are almost constrained to say of the man Christ Jesus, that He dwelleth in light whereunto no man can approach. Yet not so. Let not the humble and faithful Christian be thus discouraged. Let him not fear, in pursuance of the apostolic exhortation, to run with patience the race that is set before him, looking unto Jesus, the author and finisher of his faith. Let him not despair of gaining the mind of Christ, for this indeed is the prize of his high calling of God in Christ Jesus. And if he need yet greater encouragement, let him remember that our Lord on more than one occasion proposed to his disciples no less a model than his heavenly Father Himself. Let him bear in his heart of hearts with holy meditation and prayer those words of divine comfort, so solemnly uttered in prayer by Jesus himself: 'All things are delivered unto Me of my Father ; and no man knoweth the Son, but the Father, neither knoweth any man the Father, save the Son, and he to whomsoever the Son will reveal Him:' and those other sweet words of precept and promise: 'Take my yoke upon you, and learn of Me; for I am meek and lowly in heart : and ye shall find rest unto your souls.'

Yea verily, brethren, these are they, the meek and lowly in heart, who learn, to the saving of their souls, of Him who was meek and lowly in heart. These are they, who joyfully respond to the Lord's appeal ; 'Ye believe in God, believe also in Me. Were the materialist or the pantheist before me, I should not venture to debate with them the metaphysics of the finite and the infinite, the relative and the absolute, the many and the one, matter and spirit. I should bear in mind what David and St Paul have said of such as deny God. I should simply appeal to my own conscience, and humbly pray that in them too the inward voice might awake, by the grace of God, and make itself heard.

And what shall we say of those, who, having been taught the love of God in sending his only-begotten Son into the world, that we might live by Him, refuse to believe in Christ, while they profess to believe in God and immortality? Fain would we speak with the charity that hopeth all things of men who, unlike some of their precursors, bend reverently before the ideal beauty of our Lord's life and character, without acknowledging his divine nature and mission. But it is the tenderest and most loving of the Apostles who said: 'Whosoever denieth the Son, the same hath not the Father.' And why do they deny the Son? Because, forsooth, the dignity of reason and philosophy forbids them to believe in mysteries and miracles. As if the temple of science were not thronged with chambers of mystery, which mortal eye cannot penetrate. As if any of the Gospel wonders were more truly miraculous than the life and character of Jesus of Nazareth, than the preparation for his advent, and its mighty consequences in the world.

But let us thank Him, who over-rules all things for good, that in the unbelief of such men we have a new argument for the profound insight of Christ, and for the truth of his written Word. We still see the knowledge of Jesus Christ, and Him crucified, hidden from the wise and prudent, and revealed unto babes. We still see the foolishness of God wiser than men; that no flesh may glory in his presence, but that, if any man glory, he may glory in the Lord, even in Christ Jesus, who unto them that believe is made wisdom and righteousness and sanctification and redemption.

[NOTE.—In p. 28, l. 26 of this sermon, allusion is made to the metaphysical controversy (respecting the limits of human reason in religion) which arose in 1860 between two eminent divines now gone to their rest, Dean Mansel and Mr Maurice.],

SERMON III.

JESUS THE KING OF HIS PEOPLE.

BEFORE THE UNIVERSITY, JAN. 20, 1861.

ST MATTHEW IV. 17.

From that time Jesus began to preach, and to say, 'Repent: for the Kingdom of heaven is at hand.'

THROUGH a simple and docile childhood, a submissive and studious boyhood, having a heart even then intent upon his Father's work, Jesus had increased in wisdom and stature, and in favour with God and man. In holy silence lie the eighteen years of his youth and ripening manhood. Yet doubt we not that during those years He was guarding with prayer and meditation the temple of his soul and body, and fashioning and proving his armour against the day of trial. At length that day dawned. John, the son of Zacharias, forerunner of Him that should come, was baptizing and preaching repentance, for the Kingdom of heaven was at hand. Jesus, made under the law, had fulfilled all legal righteousness.

He must now fulfil the righteousness of the new covenant. He must submit to John's baptism, and therein be miraculously shown as the beloved Son of the Father. He must be publicly owned by the Baptist, and pointed out to a few chosen hearts as the Lamb of God, that taketh away the sins of the world. He is next summoned to that mysterious conflict in the wilderness, where the chief temptations of his earthly life were foreshown, that He might prove his spiritual strength, and, by anticipation, overcome them all. A few disciples then gather round Jesus, attracted by the power of his doctrine, and believing the Baptist's testimony concerning Him. Their faith is confirmed by his first miracle at Cana, where, by changing water into wine at the marriage-feast, He manifested forth his glory, as Lord of creation and as sanctifier of human joy, while his Gospel is symbolized as that which gives dignity to the mean, strength to the weak, and power to the spiritless. With these disciples He will attend the Passover at Jerusalem, and there become known by new signs and miracles. Returning through Samaria, He will reveal Himself to a woman of the land at Jacob's well, and prepare the hearts of that outcast race to receive in due time the fuller gospel of his salvation. He is once more in Galilee at a gloomy moment. The Baptist lies in prison, thrown there by the weak and dissolute tetrarch, Herod Antipas. The preacher of repentance is silenced. The stronger than he, the baptizer with spirit and with fire, will step into his place. From that time Jesus began to preach and to say, 'Repent: for the Kingdom of heaven is at hand.'

If, when John preached in the wilderness, there went out to him Jerusalem and all Judea, and all the region round about Jordan, and were baptized of him in Jordan, confessing their sins, what concourse would there be, when Jesus Himself preached? If the herald was so welcomed, what greeting would the King receive? To this question the sacred text affords no direct answer. But much may be inferred from the context, and something from the history of the times. The Jews in general were eagerly desiring a liberator. Swollen with national pride, they abhorred the Edomite rulers imposed on them by Rome, even as they detested the idolatrous empire of Rome itself. To them a Herod and a Tiberius were alike odious and unclean. Since the death of their first Idumean sovereign, sedition after sedition had convulsed the land, and when the mutineers found a leader to their liking, Josephus says they proclaimed him king. If a son of David offered himself to their notice, what would such a populace hope to find in him? They would look for one most mighty, one who should gird his sword upon his thigh, and ride on in majesty and glory, and whose right hand should teach him terrible things. How striking, how marvellous are the parallels of history! What the Italians felt some years ago, the Jews were feeling then! Rome was their Austria, the Herods their Ferdinand and Francis, and they looked for a military saviour, for one who should unite dismembered Palestine, reclaim Canaan for the children of Israel, the Holy Land for the people of God.

SERMON III.

But He who harangued them was Jesus of Nazareth, a man of peace: and his rallying-cry was no other than that of John: 'Repent: for the Kingdom of heaven is at hand.' He sees them writhing under a foreign yoke, and eager to shake it off; but with this He meddles not. He exhorts them to repent. He knows that their necks are bowed down and their knees enfeebled by another and a far worse yoke, the yoke of sin. The selfish and the sensual are slaves by their own compulsion. This yoke He would help them to throw off, and to that end He calls upon them to repent; to change their minds, their hearts, their hopes, their desires; to put off the old man, which is corrupt according to the deceitful lusts, and to put on the new man, which after God is created in righteousness and true holiness; to come unto the truth, and the truth shall make them free. For this purpose the Kingdom of heaven is at hand: and in Him who speaks (though He does not tell them so) they behold its King. 'Blessed are the poor in spirit; blessed are they that are persecuted for righteousness' sake: for theirs is the Kingdom of heaven.' How would such a proclamation be received by the Jews of that time? What impression would such a preacher make on the congregations of Galilee? The answer is but too obvious. A few tender and thoughtful hearts would open to his loving voice, as flowers to the sun; an Andrew prompt to trust, a Simon full of zeal, a Philip, searcher of the scriptures, a John rich in love. But from how many more would lessons such as these provoke nothing better than the idler's jest, or the drunkard's song, or the rude disdain of the reckless partizan! On this account we may see that miracles were needed to win for Jesus the popular ear, and even the confidence of his disciples. Except they see signs and wonders, they will not believe in a Prince of peace. But, in these days of ours, brethren, the person and doctrine, the life and death of Jesus, and the plan of redemption wrought by Him, should be far more powerful instruments of faith than all the special signs which were needed then: and if *we* believe not Moses and the Prophets, the Evangelists and Apostles, when they tell us of those great things, neither should we be persuaded, though the blind saw, the lame walked, and men rose from the dead before our eyes.

The more carefully we trace in the sacred narrative our Lord's wisdom and prudence in dealing with his claims to the kingly title and office, the more clearly shall we see the grandeur of his character, the more deeply shall we feel the truth of his revelation. Prophet and priest had been anointed to their functions as well as king; and we are therefore wont to say, that the name Christ applies to Jesus in each character. This is true for us; but when we observe that Messiah, that is, Christ, was then the special and proper name of that deliverer whom the Jews expected, and that in this Christ they looked for a son of David, who should restore the kingdom to Israel, it is evident that to claim the title of Christ was in effect to claim that very title which had terrified the first Herod, when the Magians appeared in Jerusalem to worship the new-born King of the Jews.

This is the reason why our Lord abstained with as much caution from declaring Himself the Christ, as from proclaiming Himself, or letting others proclaim Him, King. And yet He was the very Christ, the Holy One of God: and yet He was and is a King, the spiritual King of his faithful people. He never repudiates either title as more than his due. But He looks to times, places, persons, circumstances. What He will say or admit here, He will forbid to be reported elsewhere. And the key to this conduct is, that He will not lend his person or his name, as pretending to the earthly throne of David. Let us note this principle of our Lord in a few instances.

To the multitude He never plainly declared Himself Christ the King. If ever He was believed and accepted in this character, He owed it to the influence of his great miracles and authoritative teaching. He might have led an insurgent host in Galilee. But when they sought to make Him a king by force, he withdrew Himself into a mountain apart. True, He entered Jerusalem on the day of palms, riding upon the ass of which the prophet had spoken. True, his entry bore some resemblance to a royal procession. The people owned Him with shouts of 'Hosanna to the Son of David.' And He did not disclaim their homage. Ay! but He knew what was coming. He knew that within a few days the Hosannas would be changed for another cry, that of 'Crucify Him, crucify Him.' He knew that He was mounting not to the throne of David on Zion, but to the cross of the malefactor on Calvary.

Need I say how He dealt with the Scribes and

Pharisees, the Sadducees and Herodians? Such men were the last to whom He would have owned Himself the Messiah. It was the very confession into which they sought to entrap him; the very claim they would have inferred from some of his words or deeds, in order to tax Him with blasphemy or treason. With what exquisite skill and sagacity does he baffle their craft! He will not arbitrate in a question of property. His shall not be the tongue to sentence the adulteress. He will give them no sign but that of Jonas the prophet. Cæsar shall not be refused the dross on which his image is stamped: but to God shall be reserved the dues of God.

Occasions indeed there were, when our Lord plainly declared Himself the Messiah. But to whom? But when? To a poor Samaritan woman and her neighbours, with whom the proud contemptuous Jews had no dealings. To the High Priest and his council, when the avowal insured instant condemnation. To Pilate, the heathen judge, through whom Jesus, on the verge of death, was speaking, not to one infatuated nation, but to all nations and all times.

And what of his disciples, those little ones, who were to see and hear Him whilst He walked on earth, and to witness and work for Him when He was gone to glory? They too, zealous and attached as they generally were, shared the national prejudice. They had much to learn and unlearn. They longed for a princely conqueror who should restore the kingdom to Israel. The doctrine of a suffering Messiah was to them a hard saying. Many a grave rebuke must they receive on this score. When the sons of Zebedee desire place and precedence in his kingdom, Jesus asks if they can drink of his cup; and when love and zeal prompt the affirmative answer, they are told, the boon is not his to give; and He goes on to speak, not of crowns to be worn and homage to be received, but of humiliation to be borne by those who would be great, and of his own life to be given as a ransom for many.

And yet Jesus came to be the founder of a kingdom on earth, not of a mere school or sect: of a kingdom with subjects, with ministers, with laws, with rewards and punishments, a kingdom claiming for its lawful empire nothing less than the whole world, a kingdom faintly shadowed by that of David and Solomon, having dominion from sea to sea, and from the river unto the ends of the earth. Yes; but the kingdom of Jesus is a spiritual kingdom; its subjects are the repentant and regenerate; its blessings are in the heart, its rewards are in heaven. These great truths were, as they still are, hidden from the wise in their own conceit, as well as from the selfish and sensual. The Jews at large could not receive them in faith. Even to the disciples they were a stumbling-block till the day when the Holy Spirit enlightened and enlarged their hearts. Ever and anon they are urgent with their Master to show Himself as the Christ, the Son of David, the king of Israel. Unwittingly they do the tempter's work, and become Satans to Him they love, savouring not the things of God, but the things that be of men. So were the temptations of the wilderness daily renewed in the Saviour's earthly life;

the temptation of sense to Him who was often without food or shelter: the temptation of rashness to Him who bore all the contradictions of earth, while all the hosts of heaven were at his beck: the temptation of ambition to Him who was despised as the Nazarene and the carpenter's son, when He might have led against the Roman eagles all the forces of that East which looked for a champion; of that East which under a Mithridates had so long defied the Roman armies; of that East which had blanched the desert with the bones of Crassus and his legions; of that East which, some centuries later, subdued Asia and Africa, invaded Europe, and shook Christendom to its centre, under the flag of the false prophet of Mecca. Against such temptations, separate and combined, any one of which, faintly exhibited, is strong enough to corrupt us weak sinful creatures, unless we seek divine grace and watch unto prayer, our Saviour waged a daily warfare, and won daily victories, while He dwelt on earth, that He might be to us a High Priest touched with a sense of our infirmities. During this time, his lessons of truth and his miracles of love showed Him forth as a King of righteousness. But his throne must not be set up till a peculiar people, zealous of good works, is prepared to receive Him. The flame of zeal, which He feeds with one hand, He must damp with the other. He must be known to some as the Lord's Anointed; but He must not be proclaimed with the sound of the trumpet. He must be hidden while He is being revealed. Ejected devils must not announce Him; the sick whom He cures, the maimed whom He restores, must not, in general, spread the tidings of their benefactor. Yet his person must be known and revered; his kingdom must be preached by the twelve and the seventy; the multitudes must be moved to say, 'Is not this the Son of David?' but, when they would make Him a king, He must be found nowhere. He will satisfy no longing of the carnal heart. He will perform no royal function before the time; He will take no part in human cóntroversies; but He is ever ready to decide for God against the scorner, for truth against falsehood, for spirituality against formalism and superstition, for holiness against sin. Truly could He say to Pilate, 'My Kingdom is not of this world.'

The title chosen by Himself to veil his royal dignity was 'Son of Man': a Messianic title, it is true, and used as such by David and by Daniel: but one of humble phrase, not openly appropriating the splendour of the kingly rank. No bold questioner,—came he with honest or insidious object,—should be told by Jesus that he was Christ the King. When the Baptist, from his painful dungeon, would learn for his comfort if Jesus were indeed He that should come, the answer is not given in words. Our Lord bids the messengers report to John the mighty works they had seen. These would tell their tale to the imprisoned Baptist, and fall like dew on that holy martyr's thirsting soul.

At a later time, indeed, when the last Passover drew nigh, our Lord Himself tested the faith of his disciples, first asking them as to the various opinions of men respecting his person, and then plainly adding: 'but whom say ye that I am?' And when Peter, in the name of all, confesses that He is the Christ, the Son of the living God, He rewards the faithful speaker with a signal blessing.

The faith of the disciples in their Lord's dignity as Messiah had thus been educated, and thus tried: and now it seemed to be matured and settled. But another lesson they had yet to learn, the doctrine of a suffering Messiah. A fiery trial was yet before them, to bear up against the shame and discomfiture of the cross. No sooner have they learnt to know Christ, than their wise and loving Master will prepare them to know Him crucified. This is the next step in that apprenticeship, which is training them to become ministers of Christ, and stewards of the mysteries of God. So hard is this step, that Peter's faith shrinks from it, and he began to rebuke Jesus, saying, 'Mercy guard Thee, Lord, this shall not be unto Thee.' His hasty love denies his Master's sufferings beforehand, as his hasty fear denies his Master afterwards while He suffered. So little indeed was this lesson learnt even by those who had witnessed the mystery of the Transfiguration, that, when Jesus was taken, all his disciples forsook Him and fled. Even St John, we may deem, was led to the foot of the cross by the force of love rather than of faith. Not till Jesus, by his resurrection, triumphed over death and the grave, did He triumph also in the hearts of his disciples: nor was it till after Pentecost that the scheme of man's redemption through faith in Christ crucified was fully disclosed to them. Thus, like the Magians, they were led by grace from faith to faith, until they reached the measure of the full stature of Christ. Thus, becoming not subjects only, but also ministers of the Kingdom of God, they received and handed down the high and blessed function of discipling all nations, baptizing them in the name of the Father, and of the Son, and of the Holy Ghost.

My brethren, let us behold our King. In many aspects may we behold the Christ of God, the King of his people, while He dwelt with men. We may behold Him in the exercise of royal power, as ruler of creation, commanding winds and waves to be still, devils to come forth, the grave to give up its dead. We may behold Him as a royal legislator, setting aside a worn-out constitution, and promulgating the code of a new kingdom. We may behold Him choosing his ministers, distributing their functions, and describing their duties. We may behold Him asserting the purity of his court, when He drives the traders out of the temple. We may behold Him a royal dispenser of reward and promotion, when He promised the twelve that they should sit on twelve thrones, judging the twelve tribes of Israel. We may behold Him as a royal dispenser of punishment; symbolically, when He withered the fig-tree; allegorically, as in the parables of the pounds and the wicked husbandman; prophetically, when He denounced woes against the Pharisees and the Jewish nation. We may behold Him in the exercise of royal mercy, forgiving the sins of the paralytic and the Magdalene. We may behold a shadow of his royal glory on the mount of Transfiguration. In all these acts and functions, we may behold our divine King, while He tabernacled with men. But in the present discourse we have tried to behold Him, with reverent attention to the sacred histories, as the wise and politic Founder of a new Kingdom, in the face of a gainsaying and perverse generation.

Here we may suppose an objection to arise. Does not this politic conduct of Jesus savour a little too much of carnal shrewdness and tact, of what worldly people are pleased to call 'knowledge of the world'? The reply is clear and decisive. No, certainly not. Our Lord's conduct affords, in the first place, the highest and purest example of that great virtue, which, from Him, we call Christian prudence. Had He proclaimed Himself, or allowed others to proclaim Him the Christ, the King of Israel, of two risks He would have incurred one: the risk of falling a martyr before the due time, or that of being made, perforce, the leader of a popular insurrection. In the one case He would have been rashly challenging God's protection; in the other, He would have been taking from the creature's hand the glory which God alone has the right to confer. And so we see that this voluntary humiliation, this veiling of His majesty for awhile, was essential to the sinless character of our blessed Lord. It gives us, in the second place, the highest example of Christian obedience; for, in so acting, our Lord was obeying Law, the unerring law of God, and even the laws of erring men. And Law, as a wise and good servant of Christ tells us, is 'the clearest, and for man, in almost all cases, the safest exponent and form of Duty;' so that the true hero should realize Milton's grand description of a king : 'disciplined in the precepts and practice of temperance and sobriety, without the strong drink of injurious and excessive desires, he should grow up to a noble strength and perfection, with those his illustrious and sunny locks, the laws, waving and curling about his godlike shoulders.'

But see, moreover, to what earthly bourne this policy was leading the sinless Jesus.

History tells us of a swineherd's boy, one Felix Peretti, who by dint of genius, industry and learning, rose to the rank of Cardinal in the Church of Rome. Genius, industry and learning could give him nothing more; but more he craved, and he is said to have obtained it by other means. He began to play a part. Rebuke and censure were discarded from his lips. All his words were softer than butter, smoother than oil. He drove no traders from the temple. Profitable abuses had no dread of him. He walked before no disciples to the holy City. With feeble steps and faltering voice, head and back bent, propped upon a crutch, he seemed to be in the last stage of human decrepitude. He was not thought likely to stand long in any man's way. For these remarkable merits, as the compromise of a discordant conclave, Cardinal Montalto[1] (such was then

[1] I am not unaware that the details of Cardinal Montalto's politic conduct before he became Pope have been subject to much dispute. But the general facts seem to be established sufficiently to justify the use here made of them for the purpose of illustration.

his title) was elected Pope. Whereupon, amidst universal astonishment, he flung away his crutch, struck seven years from his supposed age, and with head erect and firm step he marched to the high altar in St Peter's Basilica: nor was any reign in papal annals more vigorous, more stern, more self-sustained, more able, than that of Sixtus the Fifth.

With this story of one who called himself Christ's vicar on earth compare the conduct of Christ Himself. Sixtus is said to have achieved his purpose by a sinful course of simulation and dissimulation. Christ wrought his work by guarding Himself from all sin. The idea of Sixtus was temporary self-sacrifice and self-abasement, against duty, without love, tending to self-exaltation: the idea of Christ was duty itself, animated by love, enduring self-abasement, kindling into self-sacrifice. Sixtus had in view the triple crown and the Vatican palace: Christ the crown of thorns and the cross of Calvary.

For again, behold your King. Behold Him who refused a crown from the Galilean populace; Him, who trained his disciples to consider him, first as the Christ, then as the Crucified; Him, who a few days before rode into the holy City, saluted and adored. Behold Him led forth by Pilate, bound, bleeding, pale, calm, silent, before another multitude, fiercely yelling, 'Crucify him, crucify him.' This was the foreknown fate for which our divine King gave Himself to be born as man in the stable at Bethlehem, to be educated in the cottage at Nazareth, to be disciplined by those years of toil and trial and suffering on earth. And why? To take away the sins of the world, to bear the iniquities of us all, your iniquities and mine, brethren, that, repenting, we might become subjects of his kingdom, sons of God, heirs of eternal life. O the dull, the hard-hearted ingratitude of men, who can behold this King, and refuse to believe and love, to worship and obey Him!

Brethren, may we repent daily, in the season now recurring and all our lives through; knowing indeed that to every one of us, for bliss or bane, the Kingdom of heaven is indeed at hand. May the holy prayer our King taught bring Him ever to our mind, evening and morning and at noonday. May we hallow the Father's name in his, and his in the Father's. May his kingdom come in our hearts by faith, that we may do his will on earth, as it is done by his angels in heaven. While our bodies eat the daily bread He gives, may our souls by faith feed on Him, the true Bread of Life. May our sins through his sacrifice be forgiven, and may we forgive for his sake. May we flee temptation after his example, and by his good Spirit be delivered from the evil here, that we may hereafter reign with Him in his kingdom of power and glory, for ever and ever. Amen.

SERMON IV.

THE INTERPRETATION OF THE BIBLE.

BEFORE THE UNIVERSITY, January 27, 1861.

---

1 Corinthians ii. 15.

The spiritual man judgeth all things.

THE special subject to which I would humbly apply this maxim of the Apostle, is the interpretation of the Bible. But as the principle which governs Interpretation governs many things else in religion, let us observe that principle itself in some of its most important phases.

If we regard man as a free moral agent, and religion as the method ordained by God to restore him to his Maker's image, lost by sin, it is evident that in every religious transaction there are two factors operating, the divine and the human. The mutual and the joint operation of these factors we cannot measure, because the divine nature and its workings lie beyond the reach of human definition. We know only what is revealed to us of them in the Word of God, and what we are allowed to see of their results in the lives and characters of men. The highest phase of this truth—the sun, as it were, from which all its exhibitions radiate—is the great doctrine of the Incarnation, very God and very man united in one Christ. The man Christ Jesus was thereby constituted the one mediator between God and man. The possibility of man's reunion with God was objectively declared, and the means of realizing it subjectively were brought within man's reach. In all these means the concurrence of the divine and human factors are again supposed. If we are saved by grace on the part of God, it is through faith on our own part. If the Spirit beareth witness, it is with our spirits. If we work out our own salvation, it is while God worketh in us both to will and to do. If we pray, it is because prayer is the voice of faith, appointed to receive the answering grace of God. And the Sacraments were ordained by Christ, partly indeed to knit his servants together by common pledges of Christian brotherhood, but partly too, as solemn acts, wherein divine grace and human faith should meet and cooperate with mysterious power and effect.

When we review the various heresies which from time to time have distracted the Christian Church, and those which yet distract it, we perceive that most of them arise from the exaggeration of one of these elements of religious truth and action, to the consequent depreciation of the other element.

Thus, in regard to the first and cardinal doctrine—the nature of our blessed Saviour—the Ebionite heresy, since called Socinian, utterly denied his divine nature;

while the Arian, Semi-Arian, and Nestorian heresies disparaged it in various degrees. On the other hand, the Doketic heresy annihilated our Lord's human nature; and the Apollinarian, Eutychian and Monotheletic heresies, severally, mutilated that human nature in some essential function. It stands to reason that all erroneous teaching in regard to the nature of our Lord and Saviour Jesus Christ, becomes, in its place and proportion, erroneous teaching in regard to that work of human redemption, which was wrought indeed, objectively as to each of us, by Him alone, but wrought by Him as very God and very Man, united in one Christ.

If we next look to the work of individual salvation, in which the divine and the human concur and cooperate, it will again appear, on the face of history, that error has arisen, generally, from the exaggeration of the one element to the disparagement of the other. Thus Pelagius overrated man's natural powers as a moral agent, and so detracted from the converting and regenerating grace of the Holy Spirit. On the other side the element of human freedom has been ignored by Calvinistic excess; and though it were improper to say that divine prescience and power have been overrated, we may say it has been forgotten that the finite mind has no measure for qualities infinitely residing in God, and no faculty of comprehending, what nevertheless it should believe, their harmonious co-existence and perfect reconciliation in Him.

The same kind of error meets us again in the opinions which have been held concerning the Sacraments. The

Romanist, on the one hand, infers grace from the outward work alone, to the neglect of human faith : the Zwinglian, on the other, treats them as mere acts of human obedience, having no promise of special grace.

What then, it will naturally be asked, is our test of truth in these questions, and what our rule of duty? Surely it is our wisdom to believe that each of these doctrines is a great and holy mystery, which we can see only in part, and concerning which we can prophesy only in part, while we are yet clothed with this body of decay and death. Surely it is our duty to accept fully, and fully, as far as we are enabled, to act upon, both those elements which Holy Scripture shows to us as coexisting and cooperating ; and not to beat our wings against the cage, wasting our moral and intellectual strength in controversies, of which we 'find no end, in wandering mazes lost.' Such controversies, alas, are often worse than unpractical; they have proved, and in some cases still prove to be 'logomachies, of which cometh envy, strife, railings, evil surmisings.' Let us escape from them by use of the clue which our Church has wisely and kindly given in her 17th Article, receiving God's promises in such wise as they be generally set forth to us in Holy Scripture, and, in our doings, following that will of God, which we have expressly declared unto us in the word of God.

There are two other important and mutually related questions of religion, in which again we have to recognize the presence of the divine and human factors, without venturing to determine the precise mode and degree in which they severally operate. These questions are the Inspiration and the Interpretation of the Holy Scriptures.

Divine Inspiration is a property, expressly ascribed by St Paul to the writings of the Old Testament, and justly inferred of those of the New, from our Saviour's promises, and from the character of the writers. Attempt has often been made, and still is made, to define the manner and extent of this Inspiration. No such attempt has been established as a norm in the Church, and we verily believe that, as elsewhere, so here, the nature of the case precludes accurate definition. The nearest approach to a rule will probably be that which shall most distinctly recognise the constant presence of the Holy Spirit with the sacred writers, without denying the free development of their human faculties in the work of authorship. 'It seemed good to the Holy Ghost and to us,' said the Apostles in their first Council; thus claiming the sanction of the Holy Ghost for the collective decision of their inspired minds, and yet expressing their individual judgments as persons who had exercised free thought and discussion.

The broad principles of Biblical Interpretation are analogous to those of Inspiration. The Bible is to be interpreted by the employment of the human faculties under divine assistance and direction. We place no limit to the use of man's learning, acuteness, and industry, as means to an end, in determining the text of the Bible, and in ascertaining its sense, grammatically, logically, historically; but after all—confronting the charge of mysticism, which we expect from the worshippers of human reason—we say that spiritual things can be fully explained by the Spirit alone: and that, consequently, none but spiritual men are qualified to form an accurate judgment of the great truths of salvation.

Let us turn our attention now to the very important passage in which my text occurs.

In his First Epistle to the Corinthians, St Paul, after reproving the Christians of Corinth for their sectarian divisions, reminds them that he himself had preached to them the plain vital doctrine of Christ and Him crucified, a stumblingblock to the Jews, who desired a sign, that is, a striking manifestation of power; and foolishness to the Greeks, who loved philosophic speculation. At Corinth St Paul had chiefly to dread the Greek error. He therefore goes on to say, that, in setting forth the doctrine of Christ and Him crucified, he had purposely abstained from the rhetorical display of mere human learning, that he might more distinctly exhibit the power of the Holy Spirit. Yet (he says) I preach a true wisdom, hidden from the great ones of this world, but revealed to Christians by the Spirit of God; for the Spirit searcheth all things, yea, the deep things of God.

The passage, which all but follows, extending from the 12th verse of the second, to the 4th verse of the third chapter, I will now venture to read, with that amount of paraphrase, and those variations from the authorized version, which are required to exhibit the view I have been led to take of its meaning.

'Now we apostles of Christ received not that inspiration which men of the world receive, making them subtle disputants, eloquent speakers and fine writers, but the inspiration which is from God; that we may know the blessings bestowed upon us by the grace of God. And these things we speak in words not taught of human wisdom, but taught of divine inspiration, explaining spiritual things to spiritual men. For the natural, that is, the merely intellectual man receiveth not the things of the Spirit of God, for they are foolishness unto him: neither can he know them, because they are to be judged in a spiritual manner. But the spiritual man is able to form a judgment on all these points, while the natural man has no power to judge him. For who, as Isaiah says, knoweth the mind or spirit of the Lord, so that he shall instruct Him? And we who are true Christians have that mind or spirit of the Lord Christ. So that no natural man can correct us. And yet, brethren, I could not speak to you as to spiritual men, but I had to speak to you as carnal men, as to infant Christians. I fed you with milk, not with meat, for hitherto ye could not bear it. Nor can ye now: for ye are yet carnal. For whereas there is among you jealousy and strife, are ye not carnal, and walking in the steps of unrenewed man?'

St Paul, in short, says that the power which the Spirit gives to a Christian is something different from mere human power: that it makes him able to understand, and, if a preacher, to explain spiritual things: but that his hearers cannot understand him, unless they too are spiritual: and, in so far as they are still carnal, they must be reared and trained in elementary doctrines like infants, till the mind of Christ be developed within them.

By the psychic or natural man St Paul means the unconverted possessor of mere human learning and science, having specially in view the Greek philosopher. He does not intend to say that the Christian can acquire no useful knowledge from an infidel (for indeed we may learn Hebrew from the Jew or Arabic from the Mahometan), but he implies that the infidel, to whom the faith and hope and love of the Christian are known only by name, can form no just notion of the Christian character, and contribute nothing to its instruction, edification and completion. In respect to Biblical interpretation, the infidel may, perchance, assist us to explain the letter, but he can throw no light on the spirit of the Bible.

Again, we find Christians themselves cited by the Apostle in this place under three several heads or classes. First, we have spiritual men who, like St Paul and his fellow-labourers, speak and explain spiritual things: next we have spiritual men to whom such things are explained, and who are competent to form a right judgment thereof: and lastly, we have infant Christians, babes in Christ, whom the Apostle could not address as spiritual, but as carnal; yet Christians still, and included among those whom, in his preface, St Paul had termed 'the church of God, called to be saints.'

Now (to speak of the last class in the first place) does not the language of St Paul in dealing with such men teach the same doctrine which we learn in our Lord's parables of the tares, the net, and the vine: the same which we deduce also from the presence of a traitor among his disciples: namely, that those who have been received into the Church, though they be carnal, are not on that account to be dealt with as heathens, but to be corrected, strengthened and restored, if so it may be, by wise and kind discipline. We should further observe, that all professing Christians are in charity to be considered and dealt with as spiritual men, except so far as they give by their walk and conduct unquestionable evidence of being carnal. St Paul does not speak to these Corinthians as being carnal and not spiritual, without stating his grounds for so speaking: 'there is jealousy and strife among you.' Never, never let us lay a snare for the conscience of a Christian brother by requiring of him any other test of spirituality than that of Christian conduct, which our Saviour has sanctioned: 'by their fruits ye shall know them.' When plain proof of carnality is absent, let us hope all things of their spiritual state, judging not, that we be not judged.

For let us not extend too widely the meaning and application of our text. A Roman Pope, Boniface VIII., had the hardihood to claim for the Roman See supreme jurisdiction in all causes, civil as well as ecclesiastical, by virtue of the maxim that 'the spiritual man judgeth all things.' His successor in these days may perhaps found upon the same maxim the right of promulgating a new dogma of Christian faith without the sanction of a general Council[1]. We mention such extravagancies only to show to what extent the Bible has been, and may be, misinterpreted by erring men. Here the term 'all things', whether it have the Greek article or not, evidently implies all those things, mentioned above, which God has freely given to them that love Him. These are the things explained by the spiritual preacher; these are the things of which the spiritual hearer can form a judgment; not the mind and the heart of a Christian brother: for God alone knoweth the hearts of men. With respect to those spiritual men, whose office it is in these times to follow St Paul and the other Apostles in explaining spiritual things to the spiritual, earnestly must we desire, earnestly should we pray, that they may be spiritual indeed, preserved by the Holy Spirit from all error and evil, guided into all truth, and enabled to preach the word with power. Yet we are not entitled to rank the very best among them—they certainly would not rank themselves—with a Paul, an Apollos and a Cephas; even as a Paul, an Apollos and a Cephas would not rank themselves with Christ. We dare not class the words of any fallible men at any time since the Apostolic age—be the speakers ever so good and wise

---

[1] The allusion here is to the dogma of 'the Immaculate Conception of the Virgin,' sanctioned by Pope Pius IX. This claim he subsequently carried to its fatal extreme, by obtaining, in 1869, the sanction of what he was pleased to call a General Council, to the doctrine (heretofore repudiated by all but the Jesuits) of Papal Infallibility.

THE INTERPRETATION OF THE BIBLE. 59

and learned and weighty—with the inspired oracles of God. When such men speak, let us hear with reverent attention, but, if doubt arise, we must search the Scriptures, as did the Beræans, to see whether these things be so. We must search the Scriptures with diligent and thoughtful study, yet with deep humility and with constant prayer. For in this work the divine and human must go together. The spiritual man alone is competent to form a correct judgment of spiritual things. By the sanctified soul the saving truths of the Gospel will be more distinctly and fully seen than by the larger learning of the merely intellectual student. Yet the admission of this principle, rightly viewed, has no tendency to discourage or disparage the value of human learning and talent and industry in the study of the Bible. For the truly spiritual man is a humble, a zealous, a conscientious man: and in each character he will neglect no means which God has placed within his reach of acquainting both himself and others with the truth as it is in Jesus.

What the means of interpretation are, and how they should be used, is a topic far too large and discursive to be fully treated here. It has, in some of its departments, been elaborately discussed by a very able contributor to a well-known volume[1]. I wish, for obvious reasons, that the treatise I speak of had appeared in a separate form. For, though it contains some things I do not agree with, and others to which I can only yield a modified assent, though, above all, it does not

[1] Essays and Reviews.

bring out, as distinctly as I could wish, the necessity of the divine element in the work of Biblical interpretation; yet it opens rich veins of truth; and many of its rules for the study, explanation, and use of the Bible are of golden excellence. Nevertheless I could not venture to recommend it in its present form as a handbook for the young student of the Bible. But for the instructor and the more advanced student it is a mine from which materials may be drawn for a fuller and more systematic manual of interpretation.

As regards the textual constitution, the grammatical and logical explanation, of the New Testament (on which points alone I should have the slightest claim, and that a very slight one, to be heard here), we must admit that new results are from time to time achieved, by improved learning and enlarged research. And, as lovers of truth (for, if not such, we are very unworthy servants of Him who is the truth as well as the life), we ought to lament that these results are so long restricted to the use of the professed divine, instead of being made, as soon as possible, the common property of Christians. Do we not still see the spurious verse of St John's first Epistle (1 John v. 7) cited as genuine by writers of slender learning, it is true, but for that very reason, perhaps, the more popular in an age of shallow reading? Is not St Paul's evidence still quoted in terms which he did not use: '*God* was manifest in the flesh'? And are not the great divine truths themselves liable to be injured by this abuse, when the student discovers that texts which he has been wont to hear cited as normal are not Biblical texts at all? Yet superficial or bigoted minds may still claim the right of quoting these texts, as long as the Church sets them before her children as genuine portions of the sacred volume.

The writer to whom I have alluded very justly cautions his readers against the idle or fallacious use of Scriptural language. One such instance I have given in the misapplication of the words of my text by Pope Boniface. But indeed of such misapplications the name is legion. What text is oftener cited and preached upon than the words 'Search the Scriptures'? yet the logic of the context requires us to read: 'Ye search the Scriptures:' and we fear the translators were dazzled by the apparent value of the imperative sense as a weapon against Romanism. 'Comparing spiritual things with spiritual'—were the words prefixed to the Sermons on Scripture coincidences by one whose memory we all revere and love. My view of the context has obliged me to render the Greek otherwise: 'explaining spiritual things to spiritual men:' as in the first verse of the 12th chapter the context again induces me to read 'spiritual persons' rather than 'spiritual things.' The value of Professor Blunt's sermons was altogether independent of his text: but his high sanction seemed to be given to an erroneous translation. Far more momentous was the error of the great Augustine, when, being ignorant of Greek, and following the Latin Vulgate, he argued the imputation of Adam's sin to his descendants from a mistranslation of the 12th verse of the 5th chapter of Romans : rendering 'in whom all sinned' instead of 'inasmuch as all sinned.'—Take another instance. The very words of St Paul in this Epistle to the Corinthians,—'we preach Christ crucified,' and again, 'I determined not to know anything among you, save Jesus Christ, and Him crucified,'—in how many Sermons have they been made a groundwork for the doctrine of the Atonement, as the great cardinal work of Christ! Yet these texts afford no basis either for that doctrine itself, or for its claim to supreme importance in Christ's redeeming work. St Paul means to aver that he has preached the truth as it is in Jesus fully and honestly, not hiding or sophisticating it to flatter human prejudice. Had his gainsayers been Sadducees, he would perhaps have said, 'we preach Christ, and him risen from the dead.' As they are proud Pharisaic Jews, and proud intellectual Greeks, he says, we preach Christ, and Him crucified, however offensive to some, and foolish to others, this doctrine of a crucified King and Saviour may appear. The great lesson which St Paul so teaches these proud men is—that of self-humiliation in face of the true power and wisdom of God: even as in his second chapter to the Philippians the lesson he teaches is that of self-sacrifice, in view of the great example of Christ. 'Let this mind, this unselfish sympathetic mind, be in you, which was also in Christ Jesus, who, subsisting in the form of God, deemed not the being like God a miser's treasure, a thing not to be parted with ; but put off his dignity by taking a servant's form, being born in human semblance: and when he was so found as a man in outward guise, He humbled himself yet further, and became submissive even unto death, and that death the shameful and bitter death of the cross.'

If we turn to the Epistle to the Romans, ch. viii. vv. 33, 34, we shall see (I venture to think) that the clauses rendered in our Version: 'It is God that justifieth,' 'it is Christ that died,' should have the interrogative form, 'Will God that justifieth' (accuse them?) 'will Christ that died' (condemn them?).

Proceeding to Philipp. iii. 16, I cannot but believe that this verse ought to be taken as a preamble to the 17th: 'Nevertheless seeing we have thus far attained (in our lessons of Christian duty)—to walk by the same rule—be ye with one consent imitators of me,' &c.

It must be admitted that some translations in our English Bible have a purely ecclesiastical character: that is, they have been accommodated to some doctrine which hearers and readers in later times would recognise, but which was certainly not recognized by those to whom the words were first spoken. Such are the passages Matth. i. 18, Luke i. 35, where the phrase 'Pneuma hagion' (holy Spirit) is rendered 'the Holy Ghost.' Whether this rendering, in the absence of the article, is ungrammatical or not, I shall not pretend to determine. Middleton condemns it. But we must surely allow it to be unhistorical. The doctrine of the Holy Trinity, and of the Holy Ghost as the Third Person in the Godhead, was not known to Joseph and Mary, who are severally addressed by the angel in these passages. By 'holy Spirit' they would naturally understand 'a divine inspiration or influence,' that 'power of the Highest,' by which the angel virtually interprets the phrase in the passage of Luke.

In Romans ix. 3—5 we read in our Bibles the following words: 'For I could wish that myself were accursed from Christ for my brethren, my kinsmen according to the flesh: who are Israelites; to whom pertaineth the adoption, and the glory, and the covenants, and the giving of the law, and the service of God, and the promises; whose are the fathers, and of whom as concerning the flesh Christ came, who is over all, God blessed for ever.' If this version be correct, then we have here the only place in which St Paul has said of our Lord Jesus Christ, in express predication, that 'He is God,' and with the strong addition and ascription, 'over all, blessed for ever.' It seems quite incredible that the Apostle would choose, for such a momentous isolated declaration, a place like this, where he is consoling the Jews by an enumeration of the special privileges which belonged to them as Jews, the last of these being that from among them should arise the Christ, the Messiah. For to suppose that the final words describe this Christ as God would then necessarily imply that the Jews expected their Messiah to be 'God over all, blessed for ever;' an expectation which they certainly did not entertain, for it would seem to them then (as it seems now) at variance with their fundamental doctrine: 'Hear, O Israel, the Lord your God is

One God.' And the modification of this doctrine in the Christian Creed Paul would surely not introduce here without some previous preparation, without some fuller explanation. This rendering we must therefore regard as one of an ecclesiastical character, adopted with too much eagerness, in order to obtain for an important doctrine of the Creed another positive sanction. But I can entertain little doubt that the words 'Christ came,' should be followed by a full stop; the next clause, an ascription of glory, being rendered, 'He who is over all is God, blessed for ever. Amen.'

Biblical criticism, my brethren, is among the most sacred duties of the Christian scholar: a duty to be discharged frankly and faithfully, as under the eye of God. Faithless criticism may be learned, may be sagacious, may often be overruled by God to expose falsehood or to suggest and illustrate truth; but as it is without the divine element, it sees and knows nothing of divine things. The blind cannot lead the blind. Faithless criticism is of the earth, earthy: it seems to flourish and flaunt for awhile, but its fashion soon passeth away. The cold and perverse rationalism of Semler and his school, the ingenious dreams of Strauss and the Hegelians—where are they now? They are gone like the chaff which the wind scattereth: and the truth, as it is in Jesus is a glad sound once more in the fatherland of Luther and Melanchthon.

The spiritual man judgeth all things. Brethren of the laity, it is your privilege and your duty to study in the Bible, to hear from the pulpit, the blessings bestowed upon you by the grace of God. Be spiritual men. So shall ye be able to judge spiritually what ye read and hear, taking heed how ye read and how ye hear. Brethren of the clergy, and ye who are looking forward to the sacred office, it is, or it may be, your high privilege and duty to explain spiritual things. Be spiritual men. So alone will ye be able to divide rightly the word of truth, and to minister grace unto your hearers.

Be spiritual men. But how? In part by humbly believing and remembering that the answer to this question is a mystery. 'The wind bloweth where it listeth, and ye hear the sound thereof, but ye cannot tell whence it cometh, or whither it goeth: even so is every man that is born of the spirit.' In part by neglecting none of the means of grace prepared for Christians in the Church of Christ—prayer, worship, and the communion of the body and blood of Christ. In part by being willing—willing in heart, willing in body, soul and mind, to do the will of the Father,—and to work out your own salvation with fear and trembling, yea with the deepest humility, because it is God that worketh in you both to will and to do of His good pleasure. In part also by remembering that spiritual grace is not given at once in its full proportion; that, to be maintained, it must be improved; that we must not stand still, if we would not go backward; that the Christian life, as described in the Epistle for this day's Service, is a race for the prize of an imperishable crown, and they who run it must be temperate in all things. Most of all must those be temperate, whose high and hard and most responsible function it is to explain spiritual things, lest that by any means, when they have preached unto others, they themselves should be cast away.

May the Holy Spirit breathe upon our distracted Church, and create in it spiritual ministers and spiritual congregations, that carnal jealousies and strifes may die away, and all things belonging to the Spirit may live and grow amongst us: that each Christian may be one with Christ, and all Christians one in Christ; and that Christ Himself, our Incarnate Mediator, our crucified Redeemer, our risen Head, our glorified and reigning King, may be All in all, to the glory of God the Father. Amen.

SERMON V.

SINFUL PARTY-SPIRIT EXEMPLIFIED IN THE JEWISH SANHEDRIM.

BEFORE HER MAJESTY'S JUDGES OF THE SALOP SPRING ASSIZE, 1849.

St Mark xiv. 55.

And the chief priests and all the council sought for witness against Jesus to put him to death; and found none.

WISELY and well has the Church appointed special seasons for the commemoration of special events in the history of the Incarnate Lord: wisely and well in each commemoration is that Lord set forth to us, not only as our Divine Redeemer, to be thankfully adored, as our Supreme Teacher, to be implicitly obeyed; but also as our great Example, that we should follow his steps. Happy we, were we not too busy, or too idle, or too proud, or too faithless, to use these instructions aright; to pursue in our religious studies and exercises the path which the Church points out; to regulate our thoughts and actions by the pattern which Christ has set.

SINFUL PARTY-SPIRIT.

In this season of Lent we are taught to commemorate our Saviour's voluntary sufferings and humiliation, from the first scene of his Temptation in the wilderness to the last crowning act of his Death and Passion. And herein, while we bless and adore his atoning love, the Church would have us humble ourselves with prayer and fasting for sin, even as He, who was without sin, humbled himself for our sakes, to the end that we, like Him, and through Him, may overcome the enemies of our souls.

At this present time, my brethren, let us consider one single scene of our Lord's humiliation, and therein one particular sin, as exhibited in the temper and conduct of his foes. And may the Holy Spirit bless this consideration to ourselves, and make it profitable for reproof, for correction, for instruction in righteousness.

Betrayed in the garden, and arrested there by the emissaries of the Jewish priests, Jesus had been led away in the dead of night, first to the house of Annas; thence, after a short delay (required, no doubt, for preparation) to the palace of Caiaphas, the High Priest. Here, says St Mark, were assembled all the chief priests and the elders and the scribes: in other words, the seventy and one members of the Sanhedrim, or Supreme Council of the Jews.

These men at length had Jesus in their power. The Reformer who had detected and exposed the prevailing abuses of Jehovah's law; the Prophet, who had sternly rebuked the inconsistencies, hypocrisies and vices of the degenerate men who sat in Moses' seat; the Son of David, who appeared as a mean carpenter's son of despised Nazareth; the King of the Jews, who came only as a Prince of Peace, whose servants would not fight against Roman dominion; the Messiah who had not been anointed with oil of their choosing; this Jesus was now in their power.

Had they studied their own sacred Scriptures apart from the glosses of false tradition and the prejudices of selfish pride, they might have discovered that *He* stood before them 'of whom Moses in the law, and the prophets, did write.' That Jesus was of Judah's tribe and of David's lineage they could not deny. Had they been willing to enquire, they might have learnt that his birthplace was not indeed Nazareth of Galilee, but that Bethlehem of Judea, 'where Christ should be born.' They might have learnt, moreover, that out of Egypt the Son had been called. They knew, too well, that the sceptre had departed from Judah, and the lawgiver from between his feet. Was it not time that Shiloh should come? And, ere they scorned his lack of royal state and power, they should have recollected that it was told to the daughter of Zion: 'Behold thy King cometh unto thee, meek, and sitting upon an ass, and a colt the foal of an ass.' No such thoughts crossed their minds. Many prophecies and types had already been fulfilled in Jesus, but more were yet to be fulfilled: and it pleased God to use the blind rage of these priests as an instrument in the execution of his everlasting purposes, to their shame and confusion. The serpent's head had been bruised, but it was not crushed: the Son of Man was yet to be lifted up; the vinegar to be drank; the garments to be parted:

his grave was to be made with the wicked: he was to lie with the rich in his death: but his soul was not to be left in hell, neither was the Holy One to see corruption: He was to ascend up on high, to lead captivity captive, and to receive gifts for men.

The transactions of the Sanhedrim thus assembled in the palace of Caiaphas we learn from St Mark, whose narrative agrees essentially with that of the other Evangelists.

'And the chief priests and all the council sought for witness against Jesus to put him to death; and found none. For many bare false witness against him, but their witness agreed not together. And there arose certain, and bare false witness against him, saying, We heard him say, I will destroy this temple that is made with hands, and within three days I will build another made without hands. But neither so did their witness agree together. And the high priest stood up in the midst, and asked Jesus, saying, Answerest thou nothing? what is it which these witness against thee? But he held his peace, and answered nothing. Again the high priest asked him, and said unto him, Art thou the Christ, the Son of the Blessed? And Jesus said, I am: and ye shall see the Son of man sitting on the right hand of power, and coming in the clouds of heaven. Then the high priest rent his clothes, and said, What need we any further witnesses? Ye have heard the blasphemy: what think ye? And they all condemned him to be guilty of death.'

As the supreme court of judicature in Israel, the

Sanhedrim thus sat in judgment upon Jesus. But the men who were here assembled as his judges had already conspired against him as his foes, and had resolved to arraign him before the Roman governor as his prosecutors. This was enough to stamp their proceedings with injustice. But, in order to the complete justification of truth, and for the warning of future ages, their guilt must become more heinous and more evident. As such it is seen in the simple and unimpassioned narrative we have read.

The members of the Sanhedrim could not justify to their own people the arraignment of a Jew before a Roman tribunal, unless that Jew should first have been condemned and excommunicated by themselves, as a breaker of the Mosaic law. Hence the necessity for this pretended trial. Trial indeed it was not: it was a judicial murder, conceived and arranged beforehand. It was hurried on with indecent haste; conducted in the dead of night, with the omission of many legal forms: false evidence had been prepared by the judges themselves. But, as truth is always consistent, falsehood seldom or never, it pleased God to confute these perjured witnesses by their own words. At length the High Priest, disconcerted by the palpable failure of his plot, and impatient to arrive at his foregone conclusion, resorts to the unusual and unjust expedient of convicting the accused out of his own mouth. He asked Jesus, in the form of adjuration, as St Matthew tells us, 'Art thou the Christ, the Son of the Blessed?' And Jesus said (the answer to such an adjuration being a legal oath), 'I am: and ye shall see the

SINFUL PARTY-SPIRIT.

Son of man sitting on the right hand of power, and coming in the clouds of heaven.' Then the High Priest rent his clothes (by that act testifying that he had heard blasphemy) and said, 'What need we any further witnesses? Ye have heard the blasphemy: what think ye? And they all condemned him to be guilty of death.' And then the Lord of all power and might is given over to the insulting cruelty of common soldiers and menials.

When we study the proceedings of these Jewish Councillors from first to last by the concurrent light of history and experience, we are at no loss to discover the evil principle which moved them. Their sin was no other than Party-spirit.

The Sanhedrim had lost the power of life and death; its ancient privileges, curtailed under the Asmonean and Edomite dynasties, had been further diminished by the Roman emperors; and, with power and privilege, the dignity and influence of its members was all but gone. For the recovery of this influence, that is to say, for their own selfish aggrandisement, and not for the honour of God and the good of their country, these councillors caballed, combined, conspired; formed a party, and acted together as a party.

At one time they had looked with hope to Jesus of Nazareth. His fame as a teacher of wisdom and a worker of miracles had reached their ears. They were aware of his popularity in Galilee, and even among the humbler classes of Judea and Jerusalem. Doubtless they would have been glad to use Him as an instrument against the hated Romans, and, when He had served their turn, to fling away the lowly Nazarene as a broken tool, according to the approved practice of worldly parties. But Jesus would not join himself to them. Nay more, He unveiled their abuses, unmasked their hypocrisies, confuted their pretexts, baffled their devices, rebuked their sins. Thenceforth they regarded Him as an enemy, who would strip them of popularity, as the Romans had taken away their power. They agreed together to destroy Him. The opposition of their more honest colleagues, a Nicodemus, a Joseph of Arimathea, was silenced by the wicked High Priest, who declared (in one sense how truly, in his sense how falsely) that 'it was expedient that one man should die for the people, and that the whole nation perish not.' Then was waged the warfare of an unscrupulous and infuriated party against one obnoxious individual. Spies were employed to entangle Him in his talk; snares were set; calumnies were circulated; all the approved tools and engines of an age which had not yet acquired the printing-press were set in motion to harass, discredit, and destroy the Saviour of the world. But from his armour of proof all their shafts fell harmless. Amidst the Hosannas of rejoicing multitudes He entered the gates of Jerusalem. Then the rage of the priests and scribes knew no bounds. Jesus must die, though by the sentence and by the hands of the detested Romans. But first He must be condemned by themselves. And this was their difficulty. To arrest Him in open day was perilous both on account of the people, and because the interference of the Roman authorities might prevent their own contemplated judgment. By night therefore

He must be taken; by night tried and condemned of them, and accused on the next morning before the Roman Procurator. The unexpected sight of means to do their ill deed hastened its execution. The traitor Judas presents himself: the bribe is offered and accepted: hasty preparations are made: witnesses suborned: the arrest effected; the trial scene performed under cover of night, not indeed with that successful hypocrisy which they designed, but at all events with that cruel issue which had been predetermined and concerted.

Have we not ground of thankfulness to that gracious Providence which has often watched over our country, when we compare a British Court of Law with the Jewish Sanhedrim of the Christian era, and our judges with the scribes and priests of degenerate Israel? The Judge of Great Britain, when he has been once invested with his high and awful functions, knows no motives but those of duty, hears no voice but that of conscience, looks to no ends but truth and right. He knows himself the representative of his sovereign's justice, and he knows moreover, as he is a Christian man, that the justice of an earthly prince is but the image of that justice, with which the King of kings rules the world. He knows himself the mouthpiece and expounder of that law, 'of which,' in Hooker's words, 'no less can be said than that her seat is the bosom of God, her voice the harmony of the world; all things in heaven and earth do her homage, the very least as feeling her care, the greatest as not exempted from her power; both angels and men, and creatures of what condition soever, though each in different sort and manner, yet all with uniform consent, admiring her as the mother of their peace and joy.'

These things the judge knows: and these principles guide his conduct. As the best and wisest men are fallible, and as many doubtful cases both of law and of fact arise, the judge may sometimes err: the bias of character or the tendency of opinion may possibly determine his mind to one or the other side of a dubious question: such things must be in a world where the clearest eyes see through a glass darkly; but God be thanked for this, the justice of our judges now abides in a region far above the atmosphere of intemperate passion or foul corruption. And with not less thankfulness we may add that of British juries the desire and endeavour is to perform faithfully the solemn promise they make to God and their country, that they will 'well and truly try and a true verdict give according to the evidence.' Scope enough there is in their functions for blameless error, and err they occasionally must and do; but we gladly believe that their decisions are usually right, and that, if ever they deflect from strict justice, their deflection generally leans to the side of mercy.

But, while we are thankful for these things, brethren, let our thankfulness be mingled with fear. Let us remember that the judges of these days not only present a bright contrast to the Jewish Sanhedrim, but that they shine not less when compared with men who filled their seats in other periods of our national history. If the names of a Jefferies and a Scroggs survive to shew their successors all that a judge should *not* be, let us dread the sin which made those unhappy men what they were:

their own unrighteous party-spirit, and the unrighteous party-spirit of their times. And if it be to a more settled constitution, to wiser laws, to enlarged education, and, above all, to the fuller diffusion of Christian doctrine, that we owe the merit of our present judicature, let us think with awe, that the high-priest of Israel had once the Urim and the Thummim; that as Israel sank and fell, so may Britain sink and fall; that a corrupt people never did, never can, possess an incorrupt judicial system: that upon the maintenance of our own moral and religious character depends the maintenance of the moral and religious tone of our courts of justice.

Yes, we thank God for it, the ermine of our judges is pure; the stream of British justice flows untainted in its channels. Yet we may not deny that party-spirit, though less coarse and turbulent than in olden days, is still so rife among us as to constitute a national sin.

What shall we say then? Is zeal forbidden? Not so: for 'it is good to be zealously affected in a good thing.' Is lukewarmness commended? God forbid: 'them that are neither hot nor cold will the Lord spew out of his mouth.' Let us therefore observe that, as there is

I. An unrighteous party-spirit, which, as Christians, we are bound to eschew;
so there is.

II. A righteous party-spirit, which, as Christians, we are bound to entertain.

I. What are the marks of an unrighteous party-spirit?

To a Christian congregation no argument need be

addressed to prove that all party-spirit is, by the nature of the case, unrighteous, which espouses the cause of evil and falsehood: all which is enlisted against the honour of God, against his eternal attributes, truth and justice and holiness; against the Gospel or the Church of his blessed Son.

But, furthermore, party-spirit in a doubtful, or even in a good cause, is unrighteous, when it proceeds from wrong motives, is exhibited in a wrong spirit, or served by wrong means. Whenever we are induced to espouse a cause, though it be the best, not by our zeal for God's glory and for the promotion of truth, justice, or holiness, but by the promptings of selfish interest or not less selfish passion : whenever we ally ourselves to a party, not because its members are the friends of righteousness, but because they are our friends, from whom, in some shape or other, we have something to hope or fear: whenever, having adopted a cause, however right, we support it without candour, without forbearance, without courtesy, without charity, or without humility; whenever, for party purposes, we employ the weapons of evil, suggestion of falsehood and suppression of truth, slander and flattery, menace and bribery, subornation and intrigue, violence and circumvention—in every and any such case we contract, in a greater or less degree according to circumstances, the guilt of unrighteous and unchristian party-spirit. And in the train of this dominant sin what crowds of ministering sins follow, we have seen in the case of the Jewish Sanhedrim. In such party-spirit indeed are involved all the darling sins of him who is said to have first raised a party in heaven against his Maker; envy, hatred, malice, and all uncharitableness. Such a party-spirit is the bane of communities: as it precipitates rash innovations, so it obstructs wise reforms and perpetuates convenient abuses; as it discourages and depresses good, so does it encourage and advance evil: and as it drives or deters pious, gentle, moderate, and humble-minded persons from interference in public business, it tends to throw the management of affairs into the hands of men whose skilful and daring genius is less subject to the controul of religious principle.

Nor is party-spirit less the bane of the Church of Christ, which it divides and subdivides into sects; and of national Churches, which it divides and subdivides into factions. This it is which teaches men to cry, 'I am of Paul, and I of Apollos, and I of Cephas;' this it is which has chiefly fulfilled the Saviour's mournful oracle, 'I am not come to send peace on earth, but a sword;' this it is which, as we have seen that it drives religion from secular life, has also, more than any other sin, breathed a secular spirit into the Church.

The sin of which we treat belongs peculiarly, though not exclusively, to the stronger sex and to mature life. Which of us, my brethren, who stand in these categories, when he reviews his past life, will find a conscience clear and undefiled by this great offence? Alas, few, I fear, very few, if any, stand free from all defilement of unchristian party-spirit in deed and in word. Great need is there that for this, as for our other sins, we humble ourselves before God with contrite and repentant hearts.

And when we consider the insidious nature of this sin, its many and unregarded approaches, its pervading influence in society, and the perils into which it leads our souls, our meditation and our prayer should be those of the Psalmist: 'Who can tell how oft he offendeth? O cleanse thou me from my secret faults, and keep back thy servant also from presumptuous sins.'

II. My brethren, if we would be most effectually secured, by the grace of God, against the influence of unchristian party-spirit, it must be by the possession of that party-spirit, which is according to righteousness and true holiness.

We are born into a world of warfare, and we bring into the world a warfare to be waged in our own souls between the Kingdom of Christ and the powers of darkness, between holiness and sin, between the spirit and the flesh, between life and death. In this warfare we have no choice but to take a part. We cannot serve two Masters. The friendship of the world is enmity against God. He that is not with Christ is against Him: he that gathereth not with Him scattereth. The seal of his baptism is on our brow; the oath of his service hath passed our lips. We are enrolled in his Church as soldiers and servants: in this contest we must be partizans. Neutrality, were it possible, would be despite to the Holy Spirit and treason against the Most High.

So then, let us follow the party of our Lord and Saviour Jesus Christ: let his name be our war-cry, his cross inscribed upon our banner. Let his holy Ark be erected in our hearts, and he Dagon of worldly party-spirit will bow down before it, and be broken. With our fellow-servants in Christ let our only rivalry be, which servant shall most richly improve the talent entrusted to his use; which shall win most souls from ignorance and irreligion to light and holiness; which shall do most to fill our schools, and empty our gaols and workhouses; to cherish and enlarge the Church in our colonies, and to gather the heathen into the true fold; which, in a word, shall have most faith and most love. And when our path is crossed, as crossed it will be in this life, by the servants of evil and the world, never let us fight them with their own weapons; this were to assure our own defeat, to give occasion to the enemies of religion to blaspheme it on our account, to be faithless to the Captain of our salvation. Never let us deem that the success of Christ's cause is bound up with our own success; but let us be always prepared to take up our cross and follow Him whithersoever He shall lead, though it be to agony, to trials, to persecutions, to scorns, to smitings, to scourgings, to death.

Be this our Christian party-spirit, that we love one another; that in our warfare with the world, the flesh and the devil, we be not overcome of evil, but that we overcome evil with good. Let Christ be the strength of our hearts: so will He be our portion for ever.

SERMON VI.

THE FEAR OF THE WORLD EXEMPLIFIED IN PONTIUS PILATE.

BEFORE HER MAJESTY'S JUDGES OF THE SALOP
SUMMER ASSIZE, 1849.

St Luke XXIII. 24.

And Pilate gave sentence that it should be as they required.

THE enemies of the Prince of Peace had achieved half their cruel work. By arresting Jesus in the dead of night, they had prevented Roman interference as well as popular uproar. By trying, or seeming to try, Him before their National Court, they had contrived to retain the form of justice while setting at nought its power. By dooming Him to be guilty of death under the law of Moses, they had placed Him out of the pale of Jewish privilege and sympathy. But the doom thus passed they could not execute. Had they dared, they would have stoned Jesus to death as a blasphemer. But the power of life and death had ceased to be theirs: it belonged only to the Roman governor. If Jesus was to die as a malefactor, He must die by sentence of a Gentile tribunal and by the forms of Gentile execution.

The Roman Procurator who then governed Judea was Pontius, surnamed Pilatus. Of this man we know little more than the Bible tells us. The name is not that of an ancient Roman house: it seems to indicate a Samnite origin. Whether he was rich or poor, whether of senatorian or of knightly parentage, whether he had risen by birth, by favour, by merit, or by their united influence, no record informs us. We know that his lot was cast in an age of fallen freedom and decayed virtue; that the religion of his country was then a mere complex of pompous rites and ceremonies without living power, that the fashionable philosophy was that which placed the chief good in worldly ease and enjoyment. We know that Pilate was a servant and dependent of the reigning Cæsar, and that this Cæsar was the jealous and gloomy Tiberius.

We may form a surer judgment of Pilate's intellectual character. The Scripture narratives show him to have possessed a large and sagacious understanding: nor can we suppose that any person of mean endowments would have been entrusted with the government of Judea, a frontier province, newly acquired, inhabited by a peculiar people, restless, turbulent, and impatient of the Gentile yoke.

The moral character of Pilate is the subject which I desire, by God's blessing, to employ for our present edification; with which view let us observe his conduct as it appears in the Gospel narratives.

As soon as morning dawned on that eventful Friday, the members of the Sanhedrim again met, and having again, with a view, probably, to the more public justification of their conduct, tempted Jesus to avow himself the Son of God, they once more pronounced Him a blasphemer, worthy of death. Then they led Him from the palace of Caiaphas to the Prætorium of Pilate, standing themselves without, from fear of ceremonial defilement during the Paschal feast. Within the Prætorium Jesus was examined by the governor, and between them occurred that memorable conversation, partly recorded by St John, which left on Pilate's mind the strong impression of his prisoner's innocence. He went out again unto the Jews and saith unto them, 'I find in Him no fault at all.' But they renewed their calumnies, saying, 'he stirreth up the people, teaching throughout all Jewry, beginning from Galilee to this place.' The mention of Galilee suggests to Pilate's mind the hope of relieving himself from an unwelcome responsibility. He asked whether the man were a Galilean, and being answered in the affirmative, he places Jesus at the disposal of Herod Antipas, who was then at Jerusalem, and whose friendship Pilate sought to recover. Herod, displeased by the Saviour's silent resignation, scorned and derided and clothed Him in mock splendour, yet he was not induced to embrue his hands for the second time in guiltless blood. He sent Jesus back to Pilate. Again Pilate convoked the chief priests and the rulers and the people, and having his own opinion fortified by that of Herod, he proposed to chastise Jesus and then release Him. He was also prompted to take this course by the remonstrance which at this time he received from his wife, who sent unto him, saying, 'have thou nothing to do with that just man; for I have suffered many things this day in a dream because of Him.' It was the custom of the Roman governors at the Paschal feast to release any prisoner whom the people named, and to grant him a full pardon. Pilate therefore hoped that the populace would demand the release of Him whom they had erewhile loved and revered as their king. Vain expectation. There lay in prison one Barabbas, probably a tool of the Jewish oligarchs, awaiting the punishment of sedition and murder. The priests instigated the people to demand this criminal's release and the crucifixion of Jesus. An infuriated mob surrounds the Prætorium. To their reason, to their equity, to their feelings the governor appeals in vain. 'Away with this man, and release unto us Barabbas;' 'crucify Him, crucify Him;' such were the cries which thundered in his ears. Pilate yielded; but not until he had taken water and washed his hands before the multitude, saying, 'I am innocent of the blood of this just person: see ye to it;' not until the people had answered, 'his blood be on us and on our children.' And Pilate gave sentence that it should be as they required. He released Barabbas, and delivered Jesus to be scourged in the first instance, and then crucified, thus unconsciously fulfilling Isaiah's prophetic description of Messiah's sufferings:—He was wounded for our transgressions; He was bruised for our iniquities; by his stripes we are healed. Still was Pilate's heart pricked by a sense of his injustice. Even now, when the Saviour had given his back to the smiter, and endured the scorns and mockeries of the Roman soldiers, he brings Him forth bleeding and crowned with thorns to those whose compassion he wished to move; and again he encounters the ferocious yell, 'crucify Him, crucify Him.' Pilate saith unto them, 'take ye Him and crucify Him; for I find no fault in Him.' And now the priests for the first time disclosed to Pilate the grounds upon which they had condemned Jesus. 'We have a law,' they said, 'and by that law He ought to die, because He made himself the Son of God.' The effect of this avowal was not according to their expectation. In order that Pilate's example might be the more memorable, his soul was thrilled for the moment with pious awe. He withdrew his prisoner and questioned Him once more. Once more his interrogations resulted in a persuasion of the Saviour's innocence, and in an earnest desire to spare his life; but his manifestation of this desire was met by the Jews with a terrible and telling menace: 'if thou let this man go, thou art not Cæsar's friend; whosoever maketh himself a king speaketh against Cæsar.' The governor's half-formed resolution died within his trembling bosom. He brought Jesus forth, and sat down on the tribunal at noon, and, for the last time appealing to the people, he said, 'shall I crucify your king?' The chief priests answered, 'we have no king but Cæsar.' Then delivered he Him therefore unto them to be crucified.

Full of interest and instruction are the scenes and characters thus brought before us. On one side we see the spotless Lamb of God, about to take away the sins of the world; on the other, that world itself, personified in its sinful children, about to shed its Saviour's blood.

The sin of party-spirit, as exhibited in the trial of our Lord before the Jewish Sanhedrim, formed the subject-matter of the sermon which it was my duty to deliver before her Majesty's Judges of the last Spring Assize. The heinous nature of this sin is seen not less clearly and strikingly in the narrative we have now read. The wicked counsellors of Israel would fain have employed Jesus as an instrument to deliver them from the Romans. Jesus had shunned their temptations, disappointed their hopes, exposed their vices, lacerated their pride. He must be extirpated, and that instantly. The struggle against Rome must be adjourned to a more convenient season. The Roman governor must first be used as an instrument to rid them of Jesus. With that odious hypocrisy which reckless partisans are never ashamed to adopt, they affect loyal feelings towards a prince whom in their hearts they detest; they charge Jesus with making himself a king, with forbidding to give tribute to Cæsar; they say to Pilate, 'if thou let this man go, thou art not Cæsar's friend'; they cry with lying lips, 'we have no king but Cæsar.' In the end designed by these bad men we see the cruelty of party-spirit: in the means employed, its baseness. And the nature of sin is ever the same. What party-spirit was then, it is still. It is the sin of a great portion of mankind; it is the sin of the world at large: not indulged alone, but avowed and justified. Necessity is the plea not of tyrants only, but of parties

SERMON VI.

also. Who wills the end, it is said, wills the means. If good means will avail, well: if not, evil must be found. If good men will help, well : if not, evil instruments must be employed, encouraged, recompensed. Is this the language of Christian men; or of those who call themselves Christ's, because Christian is for the present a fashionable name, but who are in deed and in truth enemies of Christ? Such as do evil that evil may come are the open and avowed servants of Satan. What shall we say of them who do evil that good may come? Nay, it is not we who say—an Apostle says—their condemnation is just.

But the character of the Roman Procurator is the subject chosen for our present contemplation; may it edify our souls, through God's Holy Spirit.

In Pilate, as I have already said, we discern no ordinary person.

He was not a cruel man. He would gladly have saved Jesus from the cross; and, if he scourged him severely, this seems to have been done with the hope of substituting a milder punishment for that of death. He was a husband: he could bear a wife's remonstrance. Probably he was a father. No stranger he to the gentler sympathies of the heart.

He was not a careless or indolent person. He had put down insurrection with a prompt and strong hand. He examines the cause of Jesus with care and diligence.

Sceptical indeed he was, and weak in moral faith, yet he was not an unconscientious man. His leaning was to the side of justice. Again and again he apprized the Jews that he found no fault in Jesus. Again and again he appealed to them in his favour. He urged them to accept the release of Jesus and to leave the blood-stained Barabbas in his dungeon. And when their cruel violence prevailed against his better judgment, he washed his hands before them, declaring by that vain symbol, and in words equally vain, that he was innocent of blood; that on them and theirs lay the guilt of that day's crime.

Neither was Pilate's in every respect a mean spirit. The calm dignity of Jesus, his plainness of speech, when, instead of flattering this arbiter of life and death, he said: 'thou couldest have no power at all against me, except it were given thee from above:'—these things did not irritate and prejudice Pilate against his prisoner, as they would have irritated and prejudiced a baser temper.

How it was that Pilate acquired so intimate a conviction of the Saviour's innocence we are left to guess. As a Roman, he had been accustomed to despise the laws and institutions of Moses. The priests and councillors of Jerusalem were known to him by official experience. Perhaps he had heard of Christ's benevolent miracles and pure life. Perhaps he knew that he had rebuked and baffled the ostentatious and designing Pharisees. Perhaps he saw in Jesus the foe of a degrading superstition and the champion of a better faith; and the impressions so received would be strengthened in the mind of an enlightened Roman by the simple grandeur of the Saviour's personal bearing. It may also be easily believed that in the very nature of the charges alleged by the priests, Pilate discerned the marks of falsehood. Who were these men that with loud profession of loyalty thus impeached Jesus as a traitor? The very men who most abhorred the power of Rome and designed its overthrow. Who were they that would have no king but Cæsar? Those who were ever fomenting sedition in town and country, and employing tools like Barabbas to menace and perplex the Procurator's government. Who were these that accused Jesus of perverting the people and forbidding to give tribute to Cæsar? Men who cursed the Roman impost as the symbol of their own degradation, who classed tax-gatherers with sinners, and avoided their company as a ceremonial defilement. Such accusations from such accusers were incredible on the face of them.

But, whatever the facts and reasons by which Pilate's mind acquired conviction, certain it is that he was fully convinced of our Lord's innocence. He knew that for envy the Jews had delivered him. While constrained to gratify the accusers, he cannot hide his contemptuous indignation. 'Am I a Jew?' he says: 'take ye Him and crucify Him.' And overruled by God to speak the truth in his bitter irony, he persists in styling the lowly Nazarene 'King of the Jews.' He inscribes his cross with this title; and when the priests would have the form altered, he curtly answers, 'what I have written, I have written.'

After this review of Pilate's character and conduct, we are led to ask—how came such a man to commit so great a crime? He was not cruel: why did he shed blood? He was not careless: where was now his energy? He had a conscience: why did he violate it? He valued justice: why did he pervert judgment? He could be magnanimous: why did he condescend to baseness? He knew Jesus to be without fault : why did he condemn the innocent? He knew his enemies to be false maligners: why did he lend himself to be the tool of their malice?

The reply to these questions is obvious; but dull and cold and unreflecting must be the mind which can hear it without anxiety and alarm. Pilate crucified Jesus for the sake of his own temporal and material interests. Worldly selfishness stifled the voice of conscience. The love of the world prevailed in his heart over honour, duty, justice, and mercy. As a Roman governor he desired the good will of the provincial population. Pilate was willing to gratify the Jews. Yet the desire of popularity, the love of the world, might not, it seems, have been sufficient to determine his mind to wrong. The fear of the world came in and struck the balance. 'If thou let this man go, thou art not Cæsar's friend.' Before that threat he quailed, he wavered, he yielded. He served a master whose ear was ever open to insinuation, whose soul was ever prone to suspicion ; whose suspicion was the certain harbinger of disgrace, if not of death. Yes, it must be. Jesus must die. Pilate's fortune, Pilate's safety demanded this sacrifice. The dignity of a Roman noble must not be perilled for the life of an obscure Galilean.

Brethren, these things are written for our instruction. In God's name, in Christ's stead, I, his unworthy minister, beseech you to profit by them.

In order to make the most of this memorable history for our own spiritual improvement, we must, I think, put one searching question to our own hearts. Should we, in Pilate's place, have done otherwise than Pilate did?

Accustomed as we are to link Pilate's name with the infamy of a crime, which darkened heaven and made earth tremble, many of us, I doubt not, would answer without hesitation, as Hazael to Elisha: Is thy servant a dog, that he should do this great thing? Hazael's heart deceived him: and many a self-confident Christian may first learn the deceitfulness of his own heart when the hour of temptation arrives. In Pilate we see an unjust judge: a judge made unjust not by party-spirit, as the Sanhedrim, but by worldliness, by fear of the world. England has seen evil days, when of her judges some were furious partizans, others time-serving prevaricators. Those days are gone, we trust, for ever. In these times we have no Caiaphas to violate justice, no Pilate to connive at the violation. English judges are as independent as they are impartial, not less courageous than dispassionate. We thank the Providence, which has watched over the political improvement of our country, for this, among other signal blessings, that our judges, though nominated by the executive government, are irremoveable by the same power. Assailed no longer by the temptations to which Pilate yielded, they have no Sejanus to court, as they have no Tiberius to dread.

Yet all of us, high and low, rich and poor, laity and clergy, may profit by the self-examination which my question requires. Should we, in Pilate's place, have done otherwise than Pilate did?

Pilate was a heathen in religion, devoid of Christian hope: a sceptic in philosophy, doubting the very existence of truth: a Roman soldier, prodigal of human life:

a governor, responsible for the peace of a province: a rising man of the world, over whose fortunes the sword of a dangerous calumny was suspended: a husband, in whose ruin the dearest objects of his affection would be involved.

We say this not to excuse Pilate. Pilate was in a position of moral trial; and he fell. It matters not whether he had studied the principles of justice and duty in those heathen moralists, whose works are still textbooks, or knew them only by instinct and habit. Enough that he did know them: enough that his conscience bore witness to them. By the law written on his heart he will be tried in the last day.

We speak to accuse ourselves. Let him who is free from worldliness cast the first stone at Pilate's fame. We are Christians by education and profession at least, if not in faith and hope. We have a law greater and more inspiring and more consoling than the coldly correct systems of an Aristotle or a Cicero. We have a code of morals embodied and exemplified in the life and doctrine of a sinless human being, and that human being our Creator, our Redeemer, our God. His life and doctrine teach us certain truths implying certain duties. One of these truths is, that the friendship of the world is enmity against God. And the duty is that we love not the world, neither the things that are in the world. Another truth is, that blessed are the poor in spirit, blessed they that mourn, blessed they that are reviled and persecuted for Christ's sake. And the duty is, that we fear not them that are able to kill the body, but are unable to kill the soul : that we rejoice when we are persecuted; that we deny ourselves and take up our cross and follow Christ.

If we believe God's word, brethren, we believe these truths. Are our lives conformed to these duties? Or is it otherwise with us? Do we belong to the great multitude of men-pleasers, mammon-worshippers, seekers of worldly treasure and worldly honour, living to the world alone and not unto God, teaching our children the same lore, and training them in the same paths? Is it our practice to side with strong injustice, or to connive when we do not side, and to tread down or turn our back upon the weak, even when the poor and needy hath right? Are we of those who put up with Christianity, because they find it established, so long as it is tame and cold and supple and servile, while in earnest religion of whatever form they see only an offence and a sign to be spoken against? Is it our wont to put evil for good and good for evil, to call faction principle, independence impracticability, honesty ill-temper; to commend craft and dissimulation as tact and knowledge of the world; to ridicule simplicity and sincerity as ignorance of the world and want of tact?

If such we are, brethren, assuredly we should have done, in Pilate's place, as Pilate did : but we should have done it more promptly and with less reluctance. For if we are such, we are worse, far worse than Pilate. Baptized into the name of Christ, instructed in his holy and life-giving doctrine, having before us his high example, enjoying the gift of his Holy Spirit, we swinishly trample on all these precious advantages. As faithless soldiers and servants, we forsake our Captain and our Lord; we deny Him before men; nay, by our sins we crucify the Son of God afresh and put Him to an open shame.

And if worse than Pilate, far more foolish than he. Pilate had no glimpses of the future, temporal or eternal. He knew not that he was sending his own name down the stream of time labelled with infamy. He knew not that he should one day stand a trembling culprit before the bar of Him whom he was then consigning to an unmerited and cruel death. We know that our Redeemer liveth, and that He shall stand in the latter day upon the earth; that in that day the wicked shall be cast into hell, and all the people who have loved or feared the world and forgotten God: while the righteous, who through much earthly tribulation have believed and loved and followed their Saviour, shall enter into the joy of his kingdom.

In serving the world we serve an ungrateful master. We see what Pilate did to win the world's favour. What were his gains? Deposition, disgrace, banishment, self-slaughter. For one person, whom the world crowns with the garland of success, it disappoints and disgusts thousands. Happier they, if the discipline of adversity brings them back to that Saviour, who will not cast out any who truly turn to Him, even at the eleventh hour. Happier they, though their portion were that of Lazarus, than the men of the world, who clothe themselves in purple and fine linen, and fare sumptuously every day, and at length fall asleep to wake in torments.

Brethren, if such thoughts are ever in season, most seasonable are they now. When God's judgments are in the earth, men learn wisdom. Who shall deny that at this time earth is shaken by the judgments of heaven, and reels like a drunken man and is at its wits' end? Who shall deny that it seems verily to be the almighty will of God that old things shall pass away and all things become new?

Meanwhile, that mysterious disease, herald of divine wrath or mercy, which walks the round of earth like an invisible comet, shaking pestilence and death from its horrid hair, again alarms our towns and villages, again hangs over our bed and about our paths. Unsparing, undiscriminating, it strikes down the wife with the husband, the child with the parent, the infant with the man of grey hairs, the peer with the peasant, the judge with the criminal[1].

What these things portend to the planet on which we live I know not. I am not a prophet: I can flash little light on the dim pages of unfulfilled prophecy. But this I know: that to me, to you, to all they say, Prepare. Prepare to meet your God. Set your houses in order; for it may be that ye shall die and not live. It may be that this night your souls shall be required of you.

They say: put away from you all malice and hatred and uncharitableness with all evil-speaking: be reconciled to your enemies, that ye may eat the Lord's Sacrament and be fit to die.

---

[1] The Asiatic Cholera reappeared in England during the summer of 1849; and among those whose lives it carried off was Mr Justice Coltman, one of the Judges of the Spring Assize on the Oxford Circuit.

They say: Cease to do evil, learn to do well; live not in selfish luxury: turn not your face from the beggar that lieth at your gate, full of sores; for it may be that he is accepted and you will be cast out.

They say: Loosen the bands which knit you to earth; strengthen the wings of your soul for its heavenward flight.

For all that is in the world, the lust of the flesh, and the lust of the eyes, and the pride of life, is not of the Father, but of the world. And the world passeth away, and the lust thereof; but he that doeth the will of God abideth for ever.

SERMON VII.

SOCIALISM AND CHRISTIANITY.

BEFORE THE PRESIDENT, TRUSTEES, AND FRIENDS OF
THE SALOP INFIRMARY, NOVEMBER, 1850.

St John xv. 5.
For without me ye can do nothing.

THE sickness of the world is sin. This truth the Bible teaches; and the Bible alóne has prescribed the sovereign universal remedy: 'In Christ shall all be made alive.'

The existence of the disease has never been denied; or, if ever, not now. Should we venture, in despite of conscience, to deny it, the bones of our battlefields, the walls of our prisons and poorhouses, yea, the very pavements of our cities and towns would cry out and contradict us.

Not so general is the acceptance of the remedy. Its searching properties are distasteful to the natural man. To him 'Abana and Pharphar, rivers of Damascus, are better than all the waters of Israel.' He forsakes the fountain of living waters, and hews him out 'cisterns, broken cisterns, that can hold no water.'

Among such 'broken cisterns' are the theories known by the general name of Socialism. Theories I say; for under this title many shades of opinion are comprised.

We would not employ the Christian pulpit to confute doctrines which lay the axe to the deepest foundations of society, and crush the loveliest feelings of the heart, whilst from the indulgence of self they dare to promise the increase of charity, from the emancipation of the passions, harmony and peace; good, in short, from the boundless expansion of evil.

In the name of Reason we reject such doctrines: in the name of Religion we abhor them. We say to their missionaries in our Lord's words, and in the faith and power of Him: 'Get thee behind me, Satan.'

But there are other and milder forms of Socialism, which, allowing the ties of family, and preserving, in some degree, the rights of property, propose to heal society by new executive powers, new codes of law, new modes of organizing labour and distributing wealth.

It is not within my present design to classify these forms of Socialism. I shall include in that term, for my present purpose, all parties who hope to regenerate the world by mere social organism.

These parties, so far as their writings are known to me, do not profess to regard the religion of Christ with actual disfavour: but they ignore its claim to be the divine method of universal regeneration. To them it is a venerable human system, which has done some good in its time, but being now worn out, and behind the age, must retire and make room for schemes of social improvement more wide, searching, and effectual.

In what light, on the other hand, are secular means of improvement considered by the Christian? In their right place, in just measure, in subordination to the grand principles of religion, he does not reject them. All prudent legislation, all safe association, which may smooth the march of Christianity by diminishing the evils of vice, ignorance, and destitution, the Christian will hail with gladness and support with zeal. But these are not the ground of his hope. He leans not on the arm of flesh. He knows that laws without morals are little else than a dead letter: that morals have a firm foundation in religion alone: that no religion is true, none possible, but the Gospel of Christ. He avers therefore that the words of my text were not designed for the apostles alone, not for their times only and their country; but that to priests and philosophers, princes and legislators, public men and private of all ages and all lands, the Son of God proclaims: 'Without Me ye can do nothing.'

May He who spake these words bless them to our edification.

I. We say that the end of the Socialist is a good—nay even a Christian—end, so far as he seeks to improve the condition of the poor, to distribute less unequally the gifts of Providence, to correct the immoral conventions of Society, and to smooth its harsh distinctions.

For these things the Christian also prays and labours. Is it not written that his blessed Master was anointed by the Holy Spirit to preach the Gospel to the poor; that He was sent to heal the broken-hearted, to preach deliverance to the captives, and recovery of sight to the blind, to set at liberty them that are bruised, to preach the acceptable year of the Lord? Know we not that He went about doing good; that He had not where to lay his head; that He ate with publicans and sinners; that He healed and blessed and fed the destitute; that He chose the weak things of the world to confound the mighty, and the poor of this world rich in faith, and heirs of the kingdom which He hath promised to them that love Him?

How shall the Christian not love those whom his divine Master so dearly loved? How shall he not watch and work for their good in all things, temporal as well as spiritual?

But if the ends of the Socialist are, to this extent, such as the Christian must approve, it is nevertheless certain that, in regard to means, Socialism and Christianity are at vital issue.

Socialism adopts material and outward agencies; Christianity moral and inward remedies. Socialism proclaims rights. Christianity inculcates duties. Socialism would improve men by reorganizing society. Christianity would reform society by converting its individual members. Socialism aims to abolish poverty. Christianity declares that the poor shall never cease out of the land. Socialism would divide the wealth of Dives.

Christianity glorifies the rags of Lazarus. The Socialist's hopes are of the earth, earthy. The Christian's treasure is laid up in heaven.

The Socialist, we say, relies on outward and material measures. By such methods he would resolve the grand problem of human happiness. With what prospect of success?

Granting, as we have before granted, that wise laws, institutions, and associations are essential as coefficient means, we deny that in themselves they are strong enough to secure the order, progress, and happiness of mankind. Call them, if you will, the wheels of the social engine. Say that they ease and lighten its motion. Still they are not the motive power. The motive power is the spirit of the people. Communities of men, like individual men, have as it were a body and a soul. When the soul is inert and cold, the body is a sluggish lump. When the soul is heady and passionate, the body is an instrument of disorder and confusion. When the soul is selfish and vicious, the body is a mass of corruption. When the soul glows with enlightened love, the body is an orb of light and loveliness. And where are we to seek the soul of a community? Where but in its recognition of high and eternal truth? Where but in its sentiment of duty? Where but in its fear of God? Where but in its strong enlightened religious faith?

Again. Social happiness is but the result of individual happiness. And is not individual happiness more of the mind than of the body, complex and indescribable as the mind itself? Does it not depend less on outward causes than on inward constitution and condition? How many hopes and fears and wishes, how many memories and longings and regrets, an undistinguishable throng, inhabit that mysterious circle of the human heart, and determine it to bliss or woe more powerfully than any mere outward circumstances or relations! 'Man does not live by bread alone.'

How often do we see the rich and mighty of the earth pine amidst sumptuous fare and purple and fine linen, and tremble like reeds shaken by the wind, and fly to death as a refuge from themselves! How often, on the other hand, do we see a contented mind ministering to the poor and needy a continual feast! The Pharaoh of Egypt dreams a dream upon his couch of down, and in the morning his spirit is troubled. Holy Joseph sleeps soundly on his dungeon pallet, and awakes with a light heart, for the Lord is with him.

Why is this, my brethren? It is because we belong to two worlds, the one temporal, the other eternal. The one cannot satisfy the longings of the soul. The other must be ours in faith and hope now, not only that we may have joy hereafter, but that we may have peace even here. No ways are pleasantness indeed but those of religion, no other paths are truly peace.

Or to speak of things more palpable to sense. Make institutions as perfect as you will; can you put an end to physical suffering? Can you alter the course of the world, and the organization of the body? Can you abolish disease and pain? Can you control the powers of nature, conjure the elements, and fetter the winds of heaven? Will the sea forbear to swell, the cyclone and tornado to burst, or the lightning to strike at your behest? Can you forbid the blight to lay waste our fields and the murrain our stalls, or arrest the pestilence in its depopulating march? Can you shield those you love from the destroying angel? Shall there be no more death in your new world, neither sorrow nor crying? no more widows? no more orphans? no more destitution? Can you thus seal up the fountains of human woe? You cannot. Well then; how do you propose to heal their waters? What charm have you against despondency, melancholy, despair? What lore of yours will teach us to bear the ills of life with constancy and resignation, and to rise from them with new energy and dauntless resolution? It is not you who will tell us that these things are salutary trials of our patience, or chastisements from a kind and loving Father, drawing us nearer unto Him. Such are the lessons of faith and hope and love. And faith, hope, love, are the gifts and graces of Christianity.

If we extend our view, and examine all the resources of Socialism, we shall find them, severally and collectively, unequal to the task of maintaining order, peace and happiness in the world. Particular constitutions will endure for a time, longer or shorter according to the habits of their communities. But policy the most sagacious, laws the most just, the best fiscal arrangements, the nicest adjustment of the claims of capital and labour, will collapse under the pressure of mighty exigencies, or wear out by the attrition of human selfishness. The restraints of Law alone, without some other force, material or moral, are not strong enough to bind human passions. Material force, even when adequate, when durable, when trustworthy (points ever questionable), is an evil in itself, and symptomatic of evil in the social system. We come back therefore to our axiom, that laws without morals (in the words of a wise heathen) are vain and profitless.

True, the Socialist will perhaps say. We cannot do without morals. But why must we go to another world for our morality? May we not find it within the confines of this? Has man no conscience? Has he no natural sentiments of equity and benevolence? no seeds of good, which may ripen under a wise and vigorous system of public education? no natural rights, round which all will rally from a sense of common interest?

Yes, we reply. Man has a conscience. He does retain a sense of good and evil. He does know that the one is approved of his Creator, the other condemned. But there is a force in man stronger than his conscience, even the flesh, which is corrupt according to the deceitful lusts: and this force, curbed as it may be in particular minds by various restraints, will, nevertheless, upon the whole, determine mankind at large to evil rather than to good. Neither will that intellectual culture, which a merely secular education affords, suffice to alter the direction of this force. If knowledge is power, it is not virtue, it is not happiness. It may indeed be the pioneer of both. It may, when rightly conveyed, prepare the mind for the great moral transformation we desire. But such a transformation it has no power, of itself, to work: a truth which we doubt not our Saviour designed to teach when He chose 'the foolish things of the world to confound the wise.'

And what say we to the vaunted morality of natural rights? Woe, we say, to the people who have no better morality: for they have built their rights as well as their morals on the sand. Examine the morality of rights, and you will find it to be only a sounding name for the morality of self-interest, which is, in very truth, the negation of morality itself. The morality of duties, on the contrary (without which rights have no security), is another name for the morality of self-denial, of self-renunciation: the only true morality: the morality of the Bible: the morality of Christ.

Again, therefore, we are brought to our conclusion. Laws without morals are a lifeless form. Morals take root and flourish in religion alone.

II. No: my brethren. Socialism is not destined to restore the world. It may abolish old forms: it may establish new: but it cannot endow them with a new spirit: it cannot change the heart. The *old* man will be left as he was. And what are new forms worth, if it be the old sin that works in them still? What avail new garments, when they cover only filth and leprosy? What virtue have new bottles, if they hold only bad wine?

The reform we need, then, is that of the heart. Achieve this, and other reforms will follow, in necessary consequence and due order. But how?

Hear once more the words of my text.

'Without Me ye can do nothing.'

Without Christ we can do nothing. No, surely: but *with* Christ, brethren, with Christ, not less surely, we can do everything.

And where do we find Christ? In the Bible.

Not by mere chance, we deem, is Christ called the Word of God, and the Bible also the Word of God.

God speaks to man through Christ his Word. Christ speaks to man through his Word, the Bible. Christ is in the Bible from beginning to end. Christ, we might almost say, fills the Bible. From the first words in the Mosaic narrative, to the final benediction of St John the beloved Divine, Christ is all in all. In the beginning 'all things were made by Him.' He was the consolation of fallen, dying, despairing man. He was with the Patriarch in his far pilgrimage, with Moses in the burning bush. In hope of Him the Hebrew mother rejoiced amidst her throes. Of Him psalmists sang, of Him prophets spake. Him the whole Mosaic ritual, all Jewish history, foreshadowed. Tabernacle and temple, ark and altar, victim and incense, patriarch, lawgiver and priest, warrior, judge and king, all were types of Him. He came at length in the fullness of time. Having emptied himself of the glory which He had with the Father, He was made in the likeness of men: and being found in fashion as a man, He humbled himself, and became obedient unto death, even the death of the cross. Wherefore God also hath highly exalted Him and given Him a name which is above every name, that at the name of Jesus every knee should bow, of things in heaven, and things in earth, and things under the earth; and that every tongue should confess that Jesus is the Christ, to the glory of God the Father. Having thus atoned for our sins and taken his seat in Heaven, where He ever liveth to make intercession for us, the one Mediator, through whom alone our prayers have access to the Father, He sent the promised Comforter, the Holy Spirit of grace, to enlighten and strengthen his apostles and primitive disciples for the great work before them.

Forth they went in this strength, these few poor fishermen and publicans of Galilee, to impose a new faith upon the world. And the purple of the Palatine—the stole of the Capitol—the eagles of the Prætorium—the rods of the Tribunal—the old jurisprudence of the Forum—the hoarded wisdom of Athens and Alexandria—the powers and arts and arms of world-wide empire—how did they greet those lowly missionaries? At first they took no notice, or noticed with smiles and sneers; then they persecuted, and persecuted again, and yet more hotly persecuted; at last they knelt down and worshipped by their side. And ere long, when the wild North burst its icy barriers, the barbarian swarms came forth to conquer and to be conquered; to tread on Christian necks, and to bow before the Christian's God.

And these miracles, my brethren, for miracles we may truly call them, how came they to pass? For the reason that, in spite of early corruptions, contracted first from Judaism, then from Paganism, then from superstition, priestcraft, and a faithless worldly spirit, Christ was, upon the whole, with his Church, and made that Church a fount of healing to the nations. For, in truth, if we examine the matter carefully and impartially, we shall find that to Christianity we owe all the great and peculiar blessings of modern civilization. By proclaiming the great facts and principles, that God, our common Father, is no respecter of persons; that Christ, our Redeemer, died and rose again in order that all men might be saved and come to the knowledge of the truth; that by one Spirit we are all baptized into one body, whether we be Jews or Gentiles, whether we be bond or free; that they who come to the truth are free: that this liberty may not be used as a cloak of licentiousness, for that Christians are purified to be a people zealous of good works: by proclaiming these facts and principles, Christianity has taught mankind that the only true liberty is the glorious liberty of the sons of God; that the only true equality is not that of wealth and station, but that of Christian hopes and privileges. It has placed these and all other rights under the only sure guardianship of duties: it has shewn man the just dignity of man; it has written the death-warrant of slavery; it has given woman her high sphere and mission; it has chartered a seventh day of rest for the weary and heavy-laden; it has mitigated the distinctions of race, nation, and class; and, setting all to work, as brethren, for that Kingdom of heaven in which all have an equal share, to the end that all may be perfect in their kind as their Father which is in Heaven is perfect, it has raised the standard of our common nature to an immeasurable height, and opened a glorious and boundless career of individual and social progress.

And what draws us to this House of God to-day, Christian brethren? What but the golden chain of Christianity? For Christianity, we say, has explained the true fraternal relations which connect man and man. All men, high and low, rich and poor, are brethren, bound to work together for one Master, and to help each other in that work: all to help all: but the strong more especially to help the weak, and the rich, for the same reason, to help the poor. 'Bear one another's burdens.' This golden rule of love is the very patent and scroll of Christianity. Whoso hath this world's good, and seeth his brother have need, and shutteth up his bowels of compassion from him, how dwelleth the love of God in him? And this commandment have we from Him, that he who loveth God love his brother also.

Ye, to whom I speak, are chiefly of that class to whom Providence has given more abundantly the good things of this life. 'Freely ye have received; freely give.'

* * * * * * * * * *

(*Here is omitted a passage of mere local interest, treating of the past services and present needs of the Salop Infirmary.*)

What Christianity wrought for the olden times, we have traced in faint and feeble lines. What will it do for the future?

We see the terminus of that future in the vague distance before us, bright and beautiful as the Polestar; but the depths of space between are vast, unfathomable, mysterious.

We see the Spirit poured out upon all flesh; we see the gathering of the nations: we see the kingdoms of the world melting into the One Kingdom of the Lord and of his Christ. But when? But how?

This we neither see nor surmise.

It is not for us to know the times and the seasons which the Lord hath determined by his own power. One day is with God as a thousand years, and a thousand years as one day.

Shall we be in the number of Christ's elect, we and those we love? Will our beloved country be to the end of time a chosen vessel for carrying the unadulterated seed of the word, or shall it be more tolerable for Sodom and Gomorrah in the day of judgment than for England? We cannot say.

The next question is to our own hearts.

Have we peace with God through Christ? Are we working out our own salvation with fear and trembling, the Spirit of God working in us both to will and to do of his good pleasure? If not, we are doing no good to society either as citizens or as men: for with hearts unrenewed and void of Christ we can do nothing to reform our country or our kind; rather we do all that in us lies to keep them in the bondage of ignorance and sin.

Look we to it then, that we be true servants of that Christ without whom we can do nothing.

Our country and our times are menaced by a false philosophy, which denies Christ, and a false Christianity, which dethrones and degrades Him.

From the false philosophy, with deep humility be it said, we dread less than from the spurious Christianity.

Philosophies rise upon the breakers of time, and foam and sparkle for a moment, and then dash upon the shore. Nor do we see reason to believe that a Hegel, a Strauss, or a Feuerbach will exercise more lasting influence on the human mind than many others, whose names and books survive, but whose power is of the past.

But a degenerate Christianity, nicely adapted to the corrupt tastes of the carnal man, is the very masterpiece of evil, to destroy souls and to thwart Christ: and against all such error there is great need to warn and strive, to watch and pray.

Yet,—let me say it freely, brethren; there is still more to be feared from our own fleshly lusts and habits: from the mammon-spirit which makes everything a money-question; from the Pilate-spirit which waits upon and worships the world; from the party-spirit which dwarfs all to its own low standard; from shallow sciolism, from distempered literature, from sneering, heartless, and mendacious journalism; from everything around us and within us that loveth and maketh a lie.

Against these things therefore, and against all evil, let us warn and strive and watch and pray. We are able to do all things through Christ that strengtheneth us.

Without Christ nothing. With Christ all things.

May the grace of our Lord Jesus Christ be with us all, now and ever. Amen.

SERMON VIII.

THE BALANCE OF DUTIES IN EDUCATION.

IN THE ABBEY CHURCH, BATH, ON THE OCCASION OF THE TERCENTENARY COMMEMORATION OF KING EDWARD'S SCHOOL, HELD ON THE 28TH DEC. 1853.

ST MATTHEW XXIII. 23.

These ought ye to have done, and not to leave the other undone.

THE proofs of Revelation are given in rich variety by its gracious Author, who will have all men to be saved, and to come unto the knowledge of the truth. But there are none which appeal more powerfully to an awakened conscience than the morality of the Gospel, awful in its very loveliness, and written in characters of light, which represent to us One whose thoughts are not as our thoughts, and who is 'of purer eyes than to behold iniquity.' Man, fallen creature as he is, has not lost all of his Creator's image. A moral sense belongs to him still; and, when this

SERMON VIII.

talent has been wisely used, the human mind has worked out many deep and precious truths without the help of revelation; as in our own time it has been able to calculate the elements of a planet, which telescope had never discerned. But these same truths appear in the Bible with higher sanction, larger scope, and more practical application; and they appear there in relation to other sublime truths, which, apart from revelation, could not have been even guessed. And He who has surpassed the highest heathen rule of charity, in requiring us to love our enemies, to bless them that curse us, and to do good to them that hate us; He who applied the pregnant maxim of the Stagirite [1]—'What we would learn to do, we must do to learn,' to the solution of the difficult problem of faith and works, when He said to the Jews, 'If any man will do his will, he shall know of the doctrine whether it be of God;' He who confirmed the Platonic conjecture [2] of human perfectibility, in requiring

---

[1] Aristotle, *Ethic. Nic.* II. 1. 'We acquire virtues by first practising them, as in the case of the other arts; for what we would learn and then do, we do and so learn: as by house-building men become builders, and by harp-playing harpers; so, also, by acting justly we become just, and by acting discreetly discreet, and by acting valiantly valiant.' So Pascal: 'Do you complain of your want of faith? Act as if you had it.' This is one side of the truth; the need of God's preventing and assisting grace is the other side. See Philipp. ii. 12, 13.

[2] Plato, *Theaetetus*, 176. 'If you could bring home what you say to all men, O Socrates, as you do to me, there would be more peace and less evil in the world.—Nay, Theodorus, evil cannot on the one hand perish altogether; for something oppo-

BALANCE OF DUTIES IN EDUCATION.

us to be perfect, even as our Father which is in Heaven is perfect, while He showed, what Plato could not show, how this perfection must be sought, even by abiding in Him, who is one with the Father, and by receiving from Him the Holy Spirit, who proceedeth from the Father, and guideth into all truth—who is He? Not the subtile and eloquent dialectician, holding high converse in grove, or porch, or garden; not the philosophic student, spinning his fine brain by the nightly lamp; a greater is here than Socrates or Plato, than Aristotle or Epictetus; one of fruitful and powerful discourse, but of activity more fruitful and powerful still: not a teacher of truth only, but its living example and guide; Himself the way, the truth, and the life: not a Redeemer only, but a ransom; Himself, if we do but trust Him, our strength and our salvation; Himself, if we will but love Him, our present joy and our final reward.

He who, as at this season, was born in a stable and cradled in a manger, He who grew up as a carpenter's son in a despised town of a despised province, in the midst of men who scorned Gentile learning as they abhorred Gentile customs and communion—how came Jesus of Nazareth to combine, complete, explain,

---

site to good there must ever be; nor, on the other, can it find a seat in heaven; but our mortal nature and this lower region it haunts perforce. Wherefore, we must endeavour to fly from this world to the other as soon as we can. Now that flight consists in likening ourselves to God as much as possible; and the way to be like God is to become just, and holy, and wise.'

transcend all that is wisest and best in the philosophies of the Western commonwealths? This single consideration would go far to assure us that He who, having never learned letters (if the saying of the Jews were true), nevertheless spake wisely, as never man spake, was an inspired interpreter of God. And when we further consider the power of Him who wrought so many miracles and mighty works; the benevolence of Him who went about doing good, yet had not where to lay his head; the dignity of Him who sent forth a few unlettered fishermen to win a wealthy, powerful, and reluctant world with a message of love and peace; the grandeur of Him who could purchase a kingdom of glory by obedience to a death of shame; we acknowledge in this Jesus nothing less than the immediate ambassador of God. But when He, who so spake and acted, declares that He is one with the Father; that He has power to send the Holy Spirit, to take up his life and to lay it down, to forgive sins, and to read the thoughts of men, we recognize the manifestation of incarnate Deity, and bow our knees and lift up our hearts to One who is 'the true God and eternal life.'

The sacred historians have particularly noticed our Lord's dignified presence and address. Whatever the topic or the occasion, Jesus spake as one having authority, and not as the Scribes. What, indeed, but the authority of the Son over his Father's house could entitle Him to drive the traffickers out of the temple; and what but a miraculous awe could oblige them to submit to that indignity? And, in the chapter from which my text is taken, with what authoritative solemnity does He fulminate the sentence of woe against the hypocrites who sat in Moses's seat; against the leaders and dignitaries of the high Jewish party, who strained at gnats and swallowed camels, striving with intolerant zeal for outward forms and traditional ceremonies, whilst they habitually neglected or evaded the weightier matters of the moral law. Eight times, in his inaugural sermon on the Mount, had our Lord opened his mouth to bless the humble, the meek, the merciful, the pure, the persecuted; eight times, in the close of his ministry, does He open the vials of his wrath on impenitent sinners; and, as the proclamation of blessing is wound up with a promise of gladness and reward to the persecuted children of faithful Israel, so does the array of curses conclude with a retributive sentence against the persecuting metropolis of rebellious Israel. 'O Jerusalem, Jerusalem, thy house is left unto thee desolate.' And the woes and the blessings thus solemnly pronounced by that unerring Judge, have they not been fulfilled, and are they not in course of fulfilment unto the end of time?

Having so far spoken of the moral teaching of Christ in general, and of the light which it throws on his Divine nature, I proceed to consider the particular doctrine of my text.

'Woe unto you, Scribes and Pharisees, hypocrites! for ye pay tithe of mint and anise and cumin, and have omitted the weightier matters of the law, judgment, mercy, and faith; these ought ye to have done, and not to leave the other undone.'

It is here laid to the charge of the Scribes and Pharisees, that, whilst they remember one truth, they forget another; which is one-sidedness; and, in particular, that, whilst they perform the lighter duty, they neglect the weightier; which is formalism in any case, and, in theirs, hypocrisy.

Our Lord would not have held them excused had they performed the greater duty and omitted the smaller. The Gospel has no license for little sins. 'Sin is the transgression of the law:' and 'the wages of sin is death.' 'Whosoever therefore shall break one of these least commandments, and shall teach men so, he shall be called the least in the kingdom of heaven.' 'Every idle word that men shall speak, they shall give account thereof in the day of judgment.'

We adopt, then, no fanciful or forced interpretation of holy writ, we give it no more than its just breadth and scope, when we apply our Lord's reproof, in due measure, to all one-sidedness of opinion, as well as of action; to all disparagement of truth, as well as of duty. And here we touch a vast and pregnant subject. The great heathen, whose ethical works are still our ordinary text-books, described virtue as a certain middleness, or mean between extremes. After guarding his definition from abuse, he goes on to illustrate it by many particulars, and shows how in some cases an extreme, in others, the mean, has no corresponding term in the Greek language. By an extension of this principle, equally to be guarded from abuse, we may say, that all moral truth, of doctrines as well as duties, lies between two extremes of error, and thus all erroneousness of opinion or conduct may be described as moral one-sidedness. We need not dwell upon the case of wilful sinners, whose obliquity lies in putting evil for good, and good for evil. *Their* condemnation is manifestly just. We speak of those errors which (however distantly related to sin) are not adopted against the clear warnings of an instructed conscience. Holy Scripture is a rule of doctrine and duty, but it is not a system of ethics. Its truths are sown broadcast among mankind, not drilled into the human heart; and they will be well and fruitfully received by those alone who are rich in the principles of faith and love. He that doeth the will shall know of the doctrine; shall know of it all that he need know in this imperfect state, namely, that it is of God, and, being of Him, demands to be received and obeyed implicitly. In the revelation of Scripture, as in that of nature, God, the allperfect, prophesies in part, and we, his imperfect creatures, know in part. But we know enough for the probationary purpose of God concerning us. If we know with the heart what the eye and the ear report to us, we know enough to believe, to feel, to act, to live, to improve, to grow in knowledge and in grace, until we come unto the perfect man, unto the measure of the stature of the fullness of Christ. It lies in the nature of the case that a Divine revelation should embrace truths which transcend our finite understanding, and that some of these truths, as well as the correspondent duties, should seem to be in conflict with each other. The attributes of the Most High, and their employment in relation to us, involve problems insoluble by the pure intellect, but in practice usefully exercising the faithful and loving Christian. In regard to such truths and duties, we should be guided by the admirable rule of my text. We ought to acknowledge and fulfil one class, and not to leave another unacknowledged and unfulfilled. To take a few instances from many. We ought to know and to act as knowing, that God is just, and yet that He is the justifier of them that believe in Jesus. We ought to know that by grace we are saved, through faith, and that not of ourselves, it is the gift of God; and yet ought we to be careful to maintain good works, as knowing that without holiness no man shall see the Lord. We ought to work out our own salvation with fear and trembling, as diligently as if all depended on our work, but also to be instant in prayer, as convinced that our best diligence is of no avail without the help of God, who worketh in us both to will and to do of his good pleasure.

Well had it been for the Church of Christ if this principle had been duly recognized in ages past. Well were it, if now, even at the eleventh hour, the vital acknowledgment of this truth could reconcile our jarring sects and parties. How many vexed questions, unprofitable and vain, would then find their termination.

Controversies indeed there are, earnest contentions

for the faith, of which the end is not yet; knowing no compromise, saddening and perplexing, yet very meet, right, and our bounden duty. Our struggle with sin and wickedness, with worldliness and infidelity—whether of such as know not God, or of such as deny the Lord that bought them—must be waged without truce, till 'the devil shall be cast into the lake of fire and brimstone.' And alas, what peace have we with Rome? What peace will Rome have with England while England upholds the Bible, the unadulterated Bible, and the Bible alone, as the standard of faith and the rule of life? Fain would we turn away our wearied and sorrowing eyes from the sight of wars and fightings within the pale of Christ's Church. 'O that I had wings like a dove, for then would I flee away and be at rest.' A natural longing this, but vain, and worse than vain; unscriptural even, and not void of sin. Our profession is spoken of in Scripture as a warfare; we are bidden to put on the whole armour of God, and quit ourselves as good soldiers of Him who is the captain of our salvation—of Him whose candid prophecy warned us that offences must needs come, and that He, the Prince of Peace, was 'not come to send peace on earth, but a sword.' But 'woe unto him by whom the offence cometh.' Yea, woe to England, if by her fault England has disunited the body of Christ without a cause. But if at the door of Papal Rome lie the guilt and shame of this disunion, woe to Papal Rome.

We may not pursue this controversy now. Ample

as are the materials for the illustration of my text, which the sins and errors of the mediæval Church present, we have space for a single instance only. One thing there was for which the Roman priesthood laboured from the earliest times, and labours still; unity of doctrine, discipline, and worship. So far well. Within the limits sanctioned by our Saviour and his Apostles, this ought they to have done. But there was another thing which they ought not to have left undone. I mean the preservation and diffusion of the knowledge of the holy Scriptures of God, which are able to make men wise unto salvation through faith which is in Christ Jesus. In the world of bliss we look for perfect unity, even the communion of glorified saints; here we must be content with the nearest approach to it, which can be gained without the sacrifice of vital truth. Unity is indeed a goodly thing, but in this world of trial the Word of God is goodlier still. Unity without the Bible may sink to a dead level of vicious error; the Bible, without unity, uplifts a standard of truth in the world, to which all from every side may press nearer and nearer, till it shall please their common Master to gather them together in one people for his honour and glory.

The sin of the Roman priesthood brought its punishment. Rome had depressed the Bible; the Bible recoiled from the depression, and smote Rome. It is idle to measure the English Reformation by the merits and demerits of the persons who promoted it. We may admit in their fullest extent the sins of Henry, the rapacity of his courtiers, and even the faults of Cranmer; we may allow, on the other side, the virtues of More and Fisher, without disparaging the blessedness of that revolution in the visible Church which we regard as a dispensation of Him who brings good out of evil, and bends the purposes of the wicked to execute His righteous will. At the time when the beautiful edifice in which we are worshipping was first built, in the beginning of the sixteenth century, the corruptions of the clergy, and the knowledge, of the Holy Scriptures, diffused by Wicliffe's translation, had mined the ground beneath the feet of Papal authority, and the day of reform and retribution had more than dawned.

In an age of many crimes and faults, in a court rife with guilty intrigues, the good young King, whose wise munificence we this day celebrate, and his cousin, the murdered Jane, shone like fair stars through a murky sky. It seems as though Providence had willed to bless the world with the sight of two pure models from the school of sound learning and religion, and then mercifully to withdraw them from a commonwealth which was yet to be tried in the furnace of affliction, and a church whose harvest could not be reaped till the blood of its martyrs had been amply sown.

While we recall with indignant sorrow the spoliation of Church property, which disgraced the reign of Henry and the earlier years of Edward, we thank Him who put it into the hearts of the young King and his Council to apply the residue, poor as it was, to the foundation of schools. The schools of the middle ages, generally speaking, had been part and parcel of the religious houses; and in the reckless destruction of those houses their schools perished with them. Thus were the streams of learning, which had watered the realm, cut off at the fountain-head, and new wells must now be opened for a thirsting Church and Commonwealth. Such wells were the schools of Edward.

These schools are called in their charters 'Free Grammar Schools,' that is, 'Public Schools of Literature.' When we ask what ends they were meant to answer, we shall find it convenient to state, in the first instance, what they were not designed for.

They were not professional training-schools. Theology, law, medicine, were taught in Universities or Inns of Court by professors and readers of the several faculties. They were not commercial training-schools. The apprentice learnt his craft in the workshop or the counting-house, not in the grammar-school.

For what, then, was the grammar-school designed? To educate for a common humanity and a common country: to train up boys to be good and useful men, good and useful citizens; to qualify them to adorn any station and any calling in which it might please God to place them; to make them fit to instruct, advise, assist, and guide their fellow-men, and, especially, their countrymen.

This ideal culture the Athenians called by a name signifying the combination of beauty and goodness;

the Romans termed it humanity, and the studies tending to it, humane studies; and these latter terms passed into our own language.

What then were the humane studies received into the schools of the Reformation? Chiefly the languages and literatures of Greece and Rome. It could not be otherwise. In the first place, there existed no other models for instruction in the principles of taste and beauty. Of European nations Italy alone had then a highly-advanced language and literature; and the Italian itself was but a peculiar modification of the old Italian or Latin. Europe, again, was just emerging from the influence of the Middle Ages, and those ages had treasured almost all the learning of the West in the Latin language. Latin, therefore, was not less indispensable to good education then, than it had been in any age since the Christian era. Greek was a novel study. Since the separation of the Eastern and Western empires, it had ceased to interest the statesmen of the West; since the disruption of the Greek and Latin Churches, it had ceased to occupy the divines of the Roman communion. The Scriptures were read in the Latin Vulgate; the works of Aristotle were studied in Latin translations; and these, in course of time, were superseded by the summaries of the schoolmen. But a new light of learning broke upon the Western world in the middle of the fifteenth century. The Greeks, flying before the Moslem sword, carried their literature and their manuscripts to the towns and universities of Italy, where they found kindred minds, fresh from the lore of Petrarch and Dante, prepared to welcome them, and a newly-discovered art ready to propagate their literary treasures to the utmost parts of the earth. Greek, the language of Homer, of Demosthenes, above all, of the New Testament, incorporated with the studies of Italy, soon reached Paris, Basle, Leyden, and thence, not without great resistance, it arrived in Oxford and Cambridge. At the date of Edward's charters its value, as an instrument of learning, was not fully understood; but when these charters first came into operation under Elizabeth, Greek took its place by the side of Latin as an essential portion of grammar.

The other two elements of the mediæval Trivium—rhetoric and logic—belonged to the University course, for which the mathematical and physical sciences, such as they were in those days, were also reserved.

Happily then, for England, its scholastic studies were thus determined to the languages of Rome and Greece. To these studies we are largely indebted for the growth of our own language and literature.

From that time forth the same studies, modified by experience and improved by advancing knowledge, have continued to form the staple of a liberal education. Whether wisely and profitably, was a question soon raised, and much debated in this and other countries, from the days of Milton and Locke to our own time. In Germany, towards the close of the eighteenth century, the question seemed likely to obtain a practical issue; but the efforts, earnest as they were, of Campe, Basedow, and others, to establish schools of general knowledge, entitled philanthropic or real, struggled for awhile against public distaste or indifference, and finally died away. The later plans of Pestalozzi and Fellenberg can hardly claim more general and permanent influence.

But the discussion is resumed at present in this country on economic grounds by able and earnest men, under the auspices of a powerful Society, and with the favour of persons of great public authority. All things, they say, have changed, or are changing. England, France, Germany, have each their polished language and wealthy literature. Science has conquered large domains in every direction, by research, experiment, and a wonderfully refined analysis; and there are no visible bounds to its progress. Commerce, agriculture, the arts and manufactures, have applied scientific discoveries, with other happy inventions of experience, to their own immense development. The great transatlantic continent, newly discovered, but not explored, at the date of the Reformation, is now the home and property of Europeans, occupied over half its extent by our own kinsmen, who speak our tongue, and stride with gigantic pace to the van of nations. The rich farm-lands of South Africa are ours; the vast and varied resources of the Indian peninsula are at our disposal; our flag rules from the Indus to the Irrawaddy; along every coast our ships find shelter in British harbours. Our territories in the southern hemisphere, peopled within living memory by the savage alone, are being forced to premature manhood by the detection of vast mineral wealth. We move from place to place with the four-fold speed of steam-power; we have taken for our messengers the wings of the lightning.

Amidst new facts, principles, powers, customs, thoughts—all things else being new—why, it is said, should the form and matter of education remain old and behind the time? With so much to be seen, done, learnt, remembered, and applied, in the short space of human existence, why should anybody spend his first twenty years in learning languages (if he does at last learn them) which are no longer spoken or written anywhere, and a literature belonging to the past? Above all, why should they do so who have to fight for their bread in the battle of life?

We have not stated this arduous question for the purpose of answering it now; it is complicated with too many other questions to be shortly and simply answered. A few passing remarks may, perhaps, conduce to its solution.

1. The very statement of the case implies one fact of no trifling importance. It is, that English education, to say the least, has not prevented us from taking a foremost place among the nations of the world in learning and science, in arts and arms, in wealth and power.

2. The defects of industrial instruction in this country, and the necessity of remedying them, may be broadly admitted, without allowing that it is necessary for this reason to change the existing basis of our liberal education.

3. Much as the sources of knowledge have been

multiplied and the social relations altered since the era of the Reformation, the ends of education, general and particular, may be stated as they were then: the general end, Humanity; the particular ends, Professional and Industrial training.

4. And this general end, Humanity, is it not one which the education of all classes should principally keep in view; but especially the education of those classes who have most leisure to prepare their minds for the instruction, guidance, and government of their fellow-men? And are they not in the right who consider it more conducive to this end to strengthen and discipline the mental powers in boyhood, than to load the mind with long lists of facts and names?

5. And next comes the question, whether any mental discipline be more valuable and effective than the study of language, combined with that of the laws of number, quantity, and form.

6. On which follows the further question, whether the ancient and fixed languages of Greece and Rome, with their fine forms and glorious literature, lying as they do at the root of all our civilization, and entering so deeply into our etymology, be not, in connection with our own tongue, the most perfect instruments of linguistic discipline.

7. And then, as it is admitted that all members of the community cannot have, and ought not to have, the same course of humane culture, the relation of schools and colleges to the community and to each other becomes a subject of great delicacy and import-

ance. And herein, perhaps, it is that improvement is most urgently required, and hitherto, for the most part, either unwisely attempted or unduly neglected.

We pray, then, in concluding this discourse, that those who undertake the arduous work of reforming English education may do so under an awful sense of the warning conveyed in my text. May they beware of one-sidedness ; whilst they do some things that are needful, may they not leave others undone. May they remember what is due to the Church as well as to the State, to civilization as well as to commerce, to the intellectual and moral as well as to the physical and material wants of men. Whilst they provide for the important requirements of professional, commercial, and industrial instruction, may they keep their eyes steadily fixed upon the highest standard—the true ideal—the education of the Christian scholar.

Whatsoever tends to lower that lofty standard—to corrupt that pure ideal—tends to evil unutterable, incalculable ; to the debasement of our language and literature, our faith and morals, our national character, strength and influence. A wise reformer, then, will primarily and principally consider how the education of the Christian scholar may be—not kept as it is (for we allow it to be very defective) but—improved, exalted, and refined to the uttermost ; and how progressive inprovement may be secured to future generations. And, having this end in view, he will not only deal with the matter of English education, but with its government and superintendence, with its formal and regulative discipline. This will lead him to consider the various stages of the scholar's educational progress; the preparatory school, the public school, the University; the condition and efficiency of these severally, their relations to each other, and their common relations to Church and State; the best means of improving them individually, and of insuring their harmonious co-operation for the general good. And may all be done in the fear and love of God, without whom nothing is wise, nothing is just, nothing is holy!

And us, too, who are appointed to direct the instruction of these Royal Seminaries, with our several colleagues, and all who in other schools have the same commission—may the principle of my text, by the blessing of Him who uttered it, guide us in the way of all truth and of all righteousness. May we rightly judge and honestly fulfil our duties to parents and pupils, to Church and State, to the general commonwealth, and the particular communities in which we dwell. In teaching may we be energetic and diligent, yet patient and forbearing; in discipline watchful and vigorous, yet generous and manly; in admonition earnest and faithful, yet gentle and courteous; in correction firm and just, yet kind and tender-hearted. As public men may we be zealous, according to knowledge, for every good work, without partiality and without hypocrisy, detesting party-spirit, testifying by word and deed against all that is mean and base, and false, and evil and corrupt, on the side of all that is true, and honest, and just, and pure, and lovely, and of good report; doing all we owe to all, not with eye-service, as men-pleasers, but, like the noble-hearted Arnold, simply, straightforwardly, consistently, unostentatiously, with a view to the sole service of our Heavenly Master. So, whatever judgment be meted to us here, when we rest from our labours, and our places know us no more, His blessing will await us in the day of doom, when 'the teachers shall shine as the brightness of the firmament, and they that turn many to righteousness as the stars for ever and ever.'

SERMON IX.

THE DEPARTURE OF THE AGED CHRISTIAN.

IN ST MARY'S CHURCH, SHREWSBURY, 1851,
After the Funeral of the Rev. WILLIAM GORSUCH ROWLAND,
Ordinary and Official of that Parish,

PROVERBS XVI. 31.

The hoary head is a crown of glory, if it be found in the way of righteousness.

THE Commandments of God teach the Christian not only to love his God supremely, but also to love his neighbour as himself. And such example the divine Saviour gave. He came in the flesh to all and for all that are born into this life. He bade his Apostles to go into the whole world and teach all nations. The Jew despised the Heathen, and held them unclean; but Christ taught a wiser and a better doctrine: the faith of the centurion in Capernaum, the faith of the woman of Samaria, was not less precious in his sight than that of a Nathanael or a Nicodemus. The Heathen despised and ridiculed the Jews: but Christ taught that unto the

Jew the oracles of God were committed, to the Jew salvation was first offered, afterwards to the Gentile: the light which lightened the Heathen world came forth from Judah. The high looked with scorn upon the low, the rich upon the poor: but to the poor the Gospel was preached; to the poor in spirit was given the Kingdom of Heaven. The poor envied and hated their wealthy masters: Christ by his example taught them contentment and submission. He had not where to lay his head, yet was He meek and lowly in his poverty: He bore the scorns and cruelties of the rulers of his nation even to the death of shame and torture which they prepared for Him. Even so must they who have been baptized into the Name of Christ regard and love all their fellow-Christians. To them all are brethren, all children of one Father, all the redeemed of one Saviour, all sealed by one Spirit, all heirs of one salvation. No truly Christian man will despise a Lazarus for being destitute or a Peter for having fallen. In the beggar full of sores, in the abased sinner, in the heathen savage, the Christian sees the image—defaced and darkened it may be, but still the image—of his God.

If every human being be thus entitled to respect, much more do our aged brethren claim reverence, on account of their infirmities, their experience, and the near fulfilment of their Christian hopes.

The old are entitled to our careful regard on account of their infirmities. As they have less power to protect themselves, they are more entitled to the forbearance and protection of their younger brethren. The mind of the old man is sensitive; bodily weakness and the sense of growing infirmity will account for this. Every unpleasant word, every little slight, every invasion of his rights, afflicts the old man twice as much as the young and active. He views it as an attack the more boldly made on account of his presumed weakness. Youth has its pleasures; manhood its business to engage its thoughts. Withdrawn from both these, the old man ponders on every offence more deeply. He is sometimes, it may be, capricious and ill-humoured, for age acts upon him with the power of distemper: he is suspicious, for they whom he trusted have deceived him: he is less easy to persuade, for time has made him obstinate. We perhaps complain of these things: do we know that we shall be exempt from them when old? It imports us all to treat old age with respectful indulgence: the days may come when this rule shall operate in our own favour. Happy we if our weakness then shall not be our own fault, if it shall not have arisen from causes which tend to diminish the respect entertained for us. Let us then, even for our own sakes, if not for Christ's, shew this forbearing regard to every aged person; as well to an Eli, who dreamt away his' days in sloth and idleness, as to a Simeon, who, in piety and heavenly knowledge, was the pattern of a good old age.

But there is a second and a more powerful motive for this respect. The old man has long since seen what we have yet to see; he has measured out the way which we have yet to travel. What the youth knows from the teacher's mouth or from books, the old has learnt more deeply from the experience of his own life. He has long known and observed mankind. He fancied them good, and found them evil, and often worse than he thought them in the dreams of happier hours. He deemed them evil, and he found many kind and good persons; more than Elijah found when he thought all Israel corrupt, and was told that seven thousand righteous yet remained. Thus are the old man's judgments made more grave and mild, more cautious and more certain than the unripe decisions of youth. In the business of busy life he has made many experiments, and found out what is practicable, what otherwise. He has seen wars; he has weathered tempests; he has buried brethren, parents, and it may be children; and when the young man prophecies, wisely or unwisely, of that which shall be, the old man shakes his head, and speaks with more discretion of that which has been.

Youth is strong when it rests on the experience which age has often dearly purchased. Is not Solomon guided by the Holy Ghost when he tells us in my text that the hoary head is a crown of glory? Who would esteem its experience lightly? How far must we go before we can attain to it? How much might we learn from it? Should we not listen reverently, when the hoary-headed man tells us how God has led him with a father's care from his youth up; how a saving hand was stretched forth to him in the hour of peril and temptation; how he has seen the end of the wicked and the good, the fall of the high and the raising up of the low. Will one, who has a perilous journey to make, not gladly listen to him who has already performed that journey? Will he not gladly learn of him, what to do and what to avoid, in order to reach his end in safety?

True, some hasty youth will say, if all the old were wise and good, if all were found in the way of righteousness. 'Judge not that thou be not judged.' The old man may have done much good in his day, unseen and unnoticed by your censorious eyes. His faults may seem large, yet the tears of true contrition may have blotted them from the Judge's book; a Saviour's blood may have washed the sinner's soul to the whiteness of wool. Yet true it is, and well for us to remember, that if we would receive in our old age the respect and reverence of our younger brethren, we must now in the years of our strength seek to deserve well of those around us, to do good in our generation on Christian principles, to serve our families, our friends, our country, and the Church of our God. So will the hoary head be a crown of glory to us, being found in the way of righteousness.

We should honour old age when we regard it as approaching the fulfilment of our great common hope. In every Christian man we behold an heir of glory; in the old Christian one who will soon become a glorified saint. He who to-day stands before us with grey head and palsy-shaken hands, to-morrow may have finished his course. Already he stoops towards that earth, which in a few short hours may open to receive him. To receive *him!* no: earth will receive the outward framework which decays: but the blessed self, the Christian's undecaying, ever-growing soul, returns to God who gave it. How then ought we to honour and respect the fellow-creature, who will soon be the denizen of a better world, a dweller by the fountain of light, a just man made perfect!

You know, my brethren, whither these thoughts tend. The venerable minister of this parish is gone to his long rest. His hoary head is laid in the grave, whither all of us, old and middle-aged and young, must soon follow him. Having lived on earth more than fourscore years—years, I may almost venture to say, the most wonderful and momentous since the Apostolic age—having reached that term of human life when, as the Psalmist assures us, man's strength is but labour and sorrow, he hath passed away and is gone.

Endeared to me by a friendship of more than fifteen years, during which no breath of discord ruffled the smooth current of our intercourse, I had learnt to regard him with all but filial affection. Not that we were agreed in all matters of opinion. Agreement so perfect is hardly possible between any two men; neither is it essential to friendship between those who know what is due to others as well as what is due to themselves. If any variance of opinion ever rose to the surface of our conversation, it passed away in a playful taunt or a dissentient smile.

To the members of this congregation, who will long have fresh in their mind's eye the well-known form and face—that form so reverend in dress and deportment, that face so full of kindly wisdom and mild dignity—it were needless to describe Mr Rowland. None that saw him but must have deemed him a notable man. Those who had known him longest and best knew him to be memorable for many of the noblest qualities which enrich human nature.

He was antiquarian in his studies, his tastes, his habits; and some of his strongest sympathies were with the olden time. All his attachments were stanch and sacred. His parents, his brethren, the friends and companions of his youth, his town, his school, his native parish, the quaint old house in which he was born and dwelt and died—dying, as he had often wished, in the very room which saw his birth—all were objects of his warm and faithful regard. No waverer he. Where once he had garnered up his heart, there he kept it still, if no rude shock dislodged it. No parasite he. He paid due courtesy to all: he was the firm friend of those he esteemed, in every rank of life: but his mind was too pure and too self-respectful to court the favour of the great, or bow down in the temple of Mammon.

As an unworthy minister of Him who came to seek and save the lost, as a sinner speaking to sinners, it would ill become me to exaggerate human merit, to flatter my friend even in his grave. He would have been the last to desire such unfaithfulness, the first to blame it. To say that he had his faults and errors, is only saying that he was human. His attachment to old institutions and old customs, as well as his adherence to methods approved by his own taste or his own experience, might sometimes take the form of prejudice: and his disrelish of a novel plan might sometimes be extended to the planner. When such a feeling did exist, it appeared in the outer man: for he was not of those who wear 'smiles in the eye to hide a frowning heart.' But he was no man's enemy : no idle rumours was he wont to propagate : no fair fame did he whisper away : against no man's just interests did he cabal or intrigue.

He was modest, unpretending and unostentatious in a remarkable degree. To this feeling, and to the wish expressed in accordance with this feeling, is to be assigned the privacy of his funeral and the absence from this pulpit and desk of the outward trappings of sorrow usual on so solemn and sad a day. Extensive literature he did not affect; yet in some departments, especially in old English lore, his knowledge was considerable ; and of many subjects he knew more than he was thought to know. In architecture, sculpture, painting and decorative art his judgment was excellent. Bear witness these sacred aisles, rescued by his skilful hand from long deformities, and rich with the mellow light from beautifully pictured windows, which are due, for the most part, to his bounty and his taste.

Although blest by Providence with ample store, his habits were simple, his personal wants few, his domestic expenses small. He valued money not for the sake of possessing the dross, but for the power of doing good which it gave. His heart was large, his hand free ; his bounty flowed in many channels of public and private good. His kind and delicate manner of conferring private benefits enhanced their value tenfold. His public largess could not be hidden : yet·was it ever dispensed in as quiet and unobtrusive a way as the case allowed. In improving and decorating two of our principal parish-churches—that of Holy Cross, in which he was curate for many years, and this church of St Mary, which he has filled as incumbent for nearly 24 years—in further promoting the erection and endowment of the district church of St Michael in this parish, to which he also gave a parsonage-house and land — his expenditure during life must have exceeded £10,000. I am bold to say, from my knowledge of the man, that he was moved to this outlay by the love of doing good, and by this alone. He has linked his own name to no public benefaction. His friends could never induce him to sit for his portrait or his bust.

As a parochial clergyman you knew him well. His post here was not of his own seeking. It was urged upon his acceptance by grave and good men whose authority seemed to him the voice of Providence. That he performed the duties so acquired in the way which conscience prompted and ability permitted, those who knew him intimately do not for an instant doubt. His public bounty has been named already. You know all that he has done for this sacred edifice: you know what he has done for our daughter church of St Michael. You know with how large a liberality he supported and improved our parochial schools. Some of you know that his private charities were not less large and liberal. Often has his seasonable and ever delicate kindness dried the orphan's tears, and made the widow's heart to sing for joy.

His great age and growing infirmities did not interrupt the punctual discharge of his usual duties to the very day when he was seized with fatal illness. He had for some years retired, generally, from the work of preaching, on account of the declining powers of a voice which was never strong. In the reading desk he was ever assiduous: at the holy Table of the Lord he never failed to take his proper place.

Some persons, who find a strange pleasure in disparaging goodness, have objected to my venerated friend's character as a clergyman, that he neglected the important duty of visiting the poor in their own dwellings.

To this objection, when I have had the opportunity of replying, my reply has ever been this: 'It is true that visiting the poor at their houses is among the most important duties of a parish clergyman. It is true that Mr Rowland, though neither disparaging this duty nor altogether avoiding it, did not carry on the daily work of personal visitation. Two reasons, I believe, combined to withhold him: first, a sense of that personal infirmity of deafness, which seriously impeded his familiar converse with his fellow-men; and next, a very nice, and, if you will, an over-refined delicacy of sentiment, which made him shrink from intruding unasked and, it might be, unwished into the dwellings of the poor, whose feelings and rights he held no less sacred than those of their rich neighbours. He thought, I doubt not, in regard to this work of visiting, that zeal untempered by discretion may do more harm than good; and he probably distrusted his own possession of that great and rare gift— that union of physical and moral qualities, that harmony of principle and temperament, of habits and manners,— which alone, by God's grace, can fit a man to perform well a work so great and so difficult. All he could do, or all he thought he could do with advantage, he did not leave undone. The provision he made for the good of his poor by schools, by private benefactions, and by engaging two curates to discharge duties to which he was himself unequal, absorbed all, or nearly all, the revenues of his benefice. And if it be said that without personal visitation he could not tell how to distribute his alms wisely and justly—allowing much force to this remark, I yet reply, that, besides the confidence due to the reports of his curates, he happily possessed in his vestry-clerk and overseer a referee on all matters concerning the inhabitants of this parish, whose accurate knowledge could be questioned as little as his integrity and humanity.' I repeat then that, as a parochial minister, Mr Rowland did what he could, in no niggard and in no narrow spirit. Of such a man who would not say, with the kind-hearted erring minstrel,

> Be to his faults a little blind;
> be to his virtues very kind?

Personal religion was too sacred with him to be the subject of public profession or everyday conversation. From profession and proclamation of any kind he was indeed instinctively, habitually, strongly averse. The blessed Saviour, whose minister he was and whose beneficent kindness he imitated, he could not but have loved. Being mild and charitable, humble and upright, I believe that he sanctified the Lord God in his heart.

Nevertheless we judge nothing before the time, until the Lord come, who shall bring to light the hidden things of darkness, and make manifest the counsels of the heart: and then shall every man have praise of God.

One trait more, and I have done. He loved all that is beautiful in nature and in art: he loved children, he loved flowers: no slight indications these of a pure and gentle spirit. His last gift to one whom he honoured with his regard was a bunch of the flowers he knew she prized, the myrtles of her native climate.

I know not how it may be with other households; but in mine the dear good old man will be long and sadly missed by all its inmates. Long and sadly will that feeling haunt us, which our greatest living poet describes:

> So much the vital spirits sink
> to see the vacant chair, and think
> how good! how kind! and he is gone.

Christian brethren, God's will be done. He is gone, we follow. If we live to be hoary-headed, may we be found in the way of righteousness. May we live unto the Lord and not unto men; so, whensoever the fatal hour shall come, we shall die the death of the righteous, and our last end will be like his.

SERMON X.

AT THE ORDINATION HELD IN HIS CATHEDRAL CHURCH BY THE RIGHT REV. E. HAROLD BROWNE, D.D. LORD BISHOP OF ELY, ON TRINITY SUNDAY, 1867.

St John xv. 26, 27.

But when the Comforter is come, whom I will send unto you from the Father, even the Spirit of Truth, which proceedeth from the Father, He shall testify of me. And ye also shall bear witness, because ye have been with me from the beginning.

ON this passage, more perhaps than on any one other place of Holy Writ, rests our recognition of that great mystery of godliness which the Church this day commemorates, and from which the remaining Sundays of the Christian year are named—the Doctrine of a Trinity of Persons in the Unity of the Divine Nature. The Eastern Church indeed has confined its exposition of that Doctrine to the formula here given. The Holy Ghost, the Spirit of Truth, proceeds from the Father. But the Western Church, having regard to the intimate union of the Father and the Son, as set forth by our Lord himself in this Paschal discourse, and to the further fact that the Holy Spirit is called indifferently by St Paul the Spirit of God, the Spirit of Christ and the Spirit of Him that raised up Jesus from the dead, declares the procession of the Holy Ghost to be from the Father and the Son. And this decision is supported by the consideration that, as the Spirit is here said to proceed only from the Father, so He is said to be sent only by the Son : yet the sending of the Spirit is by all admitted to be the co-equal act of the Father and the Son, even as our Lord had before said (xiv. 26), 'But the Comforter, which is the Holy Ghost, whom the Father will send in my name, He shall teach you all things.' In my text, therefore, his design was to repeat a consoling truth to his disciples, not to formulate a dogma: and, as the Holy Spirit is sent alike by the Father and the Son, so may He be justly said to proceed alike from the Father and the Son.

It is far from my mind, brethren, to disparage the accurate formulation of dogma. On the contrary, I hold that wherever definition is needful, accuracy of definition is needful : and I grant that definite dogma is often needed to secure sound doctrine. With the mouth confession is made unto salvation, and the difference of a single word, nay of a single syllable, possibly of a single letter, may constitute the distinction between God's saving truth and the devil's ruinous lie. When we say, *Christus homo verus est*, Christ is very man, we recite an essential article of faith. But were we to say, *Christus homo merus est,* Christ is mere man, we should deny the faith of the Son of God, who loved us and gave himself for us.

But, while we say that accuracy is always necessary to definition, we would not also say that definition itself is necessary on every point of religious doctrine. While we accept the propositions of our own three Creeds as consonant with the language of Scripture, none of us, I trust, will affirm that the absence of the words Filioque—'and the Son'—from the Eastern text of the Nicene Creed brands the Eastern Church and all its members with damnable error. And some, perhaps, may think that negative propositions, such as 'the Father uncreate, the Son uncreate, and the Holy Ghost uncreate,' were sufficient to guard from error our conception of the triune mode of being in the divine essence, without using, as formal dogmas, the positive terms 'begotten' and 'proceeding,' which add nothing to the reality of our conception, while in Scripture they stand as isolated expressions, employed to illustrate rather than to define.

The time is not yet come, it is probably far distant, in which our divine Head will enable his Church to revise and digest its formal standards of dogmatic truth: but to pray for the coming of that time, and with that prayer to combine the careful study of our formularies in the light of divine revelation and in the spirit of divine love, this, surely, is an edifying work for every Minister of Christ, and one which will strengthen him for the edification of Christ's flock.

But to return to my text.

He who is the Third Person in the Divine Trinity, the Holy Ghost, here called the Paraclete or Comforter, the Spirit of truth, He, (Christ himself says,) shall bear witness of Christ; and Christ's Apostles shall bear witness. The Holy Ghost, descending on the day of Pentecost, shall testify to the Apostles themselves, teaching them all things, and bringing all things to their remembrance. And in this power the Apostles shall testify. Who so fit to be Christ's witnesses to the world, as they who have been with Christ from the beginning of his ministry? Though Jesus paused here, we, brethren, are privileged to carry forward his promise, comparing Scripture with Scripture, reason with fact. This commission was not to end with the Apostles: how could it be so, if the mustard-seed was to become a tree, and to overshadow all nations? They were to ordain others to the same commission; conveying to them the power they themselves possessed to baptize, convert, teach and ordain, according to the differences of administrations approved in the Church by their authority. And the Holy Ghost who first testified to them of Christ would continue that testimony to their successors, shedding abroad indeed in the hearts of all faithful men, but peculiarly in the hearts of faithful ministers, that love of Christ which alone is the testimony and the power and the light and the life of God in the human soul.

Who then were to be thus commissioned? Who were to be—who *are*—the lawfully ordained ministers of Christ? God, says St Paul to the Corinthians, hath set some in the Church; first apostles, secondly prophets, thirdly teachers, after that miracles, then gifts of healings, helps, governments, diversities of tongues. Apostles died out: prophets and diversities of tongues came to an end: miracles and gifts of healings were withdrawn: but governments, teachers, and helps remained in the Church and yet remain as the three ministerial orders of Bishops, Priests, and Deacons.

Well may we rejoice and be thankful, brethren, that we possess a ministry thus divinely founded, thus apostolically descended, thus scripturally certified, thus commissioned and continued through eighteen centuries to the present day: a ministry whose line is gone out through all the earth, and their words to the end of the world. But our rejoicing is tempered with sorrow and shame and humiliation when, looking back through those centuries, we find that a Church so gloriously endowed did not keep itself free from the taints of worldliness and error: that the faithful city became an harlot: that, when at length flagrant corruption called aloud for reformation, reformation could not be wrought without schism, of which the guilt be theirs who call falsehood truth and truth falsehood, who put darkness for light and light for darkness. But we have yet nearer and more urgent cause of sorrow. For the divisions of our own reformed Church we have great searchings of heart. They grow out of questions in which truth and error lie so near each other, theory and practice so wide apart, that to clergymen of every grade, from the bishop to the curate, the exact path of duty is hard to find, though they seek it with conscientious aim; hard to keep, though they strive with earnest prayer. Two schools of religious thought exist amongst us from the Reformation to the present hour: two chief schools, I mean, since many there are, especially in these latter days, who take their standpoint of theory and practice between the two. The wise policy of our Reformers designed to include both schools in one common form of worship; and bitter experience has shown that every departure from that policy brings some disastrous consequences; first, rebellion, then revolution, then angry and oppressive reaction, resulting in settled and spreading schism. Where, on each of these occasions, was that tempering of the wisdom of the serpent with the harmlessness of the dove, which our blessed Lord recommended to his disciples? Where was wise moderation, where charitable forbearance, where reasonable concession? Forgotten all; nay rather, spurned all and set aside by the violence of party zeal. And is it in the doom of our fallen race that the plain warnings of experience shall never teach, never restrain, never guide us? Do we suppose that an enterprize, which wrecked the altar and the throne in the 17th century, can be renewed with any chance of success in days which, if less fanatical, are surely not more submissive to authority? Do we suppose that the laity in general will accept, as the established form of worship, a ritual expressly designed to symbolize the power and dignity of the priestly office as mediative between God and man in conferring the highest gifts of grace? I think not; my sense of honesty compels me to add, I hope not. But I refrain from pursuing a subject which our gracious Sovereign has committed to the joint consideration of many able and eminent men, lay as well as clerical. May their thoughtful investigation and deliberate advice be blest to the peace of the Church and the welfare of this nation.

Have I then any sympathy with the sour and narrow principles of those who would forbid us to beautify the sanctuary and service of God? None whatever. True it is, in the language of Heber's fine hymn, that the heart's adoration, the prayers of the poor in spirit, are richer in themselves and dearer to God than all the wealth of earth and ocean. True it is that God may be as acceptably worshipped by holy hearts and simple voices on the hillside beneath the canopy of heaven as in this grand temple,

> Where through the long-drawn aisle and fretted vault
> The pealing anthem swells the notes of praise.

But it is not less true that, as man has received from God, in whose image he was created, a sense of the beautiful, and skill to represent the beautiful to the eye and ear in works of art and strains of music, so is he privileged, so has he ever been accustomed, as Scripture shews, to declare his gratitude for these good gifts by dedicating their noblest fruits to the honour and glory and public service of the Giver.

Am I justly chargeable with detracting from the true dignity of the ministerial office? God forbid. Have I not already said that we derive our line of orders from the apostles? If so, we are, with St Paul, ministers of Christ and stewards of the mysteries of God. But then, look at St Paul's first and immediate inference. 'It is required in stewards, that a man be found faithful.' Brethren, let us be faithful. Let us prove our apostolic descent by doing apostolic work; by testifying of Christ in the power of the Holy Ghost. We need not be for ever talking of our apostolic descent. One of our bishops has wisely said that this is a weapon better kept in the scabbard for the season of defence than brandished with frequent demonstration before the public eye. And what power of godliness, what use of edification resides in those many-named, many-shaped, many-coloured, and ever-varying distinctions of clerical attire, which, if they attract some worshippers to prayer and communion, repel, alas, a far larger number of sincere Christian people?

At a great and momentous congress of the European states in the early part of this century, the ambassador of England was distinguished by the total absence of external decoration amidst the general glare of stars and ribands. Did the simplicity of his style make him less respected or less influential? did he less effectually perform the work he was sent to do? Assuredly not. He represented a great power: he had a great mission to execute: herein lay his dignity and his influence. And we, brethren, we are ambassadors for Christ. Let us with all godly simplicity fulfil our great and glorious—our arduous and responsible—embassy; not magnifying our own office, yet speaking to God's erring children, as though God did beseech them by us to return and repent:

praying all miserable sinners in Christ's stead, 'be ye reconciled to God.'

For this purpose is the Holy Spirit given in larger measure to them that minister in holy things in the Church, that, growing in grace themselves and in the knowledge of the truth, they may teach others and stablish them in all goodness: that, being in Christ themselves, they may bring others to Christ, and instruct them to abide in his fellowship, by a faithful, earnest and intelligent use of all the appointed means of grace, the study of God's word, private and public prayer, and the frequent communion of their Saviour's body and blood. If the ministers of Christ thus lay a sure foundation in the hearts of their flock, they may humbly but firmly trust that the Lord himself will build thereupon the fabric of holiness in all its beauty.

Our lot is indeed cast in strange and troublous times. That pure and apostolic branch of the Church Catholic to which we belong will have duties more than ever difficult, more than ever momentous to this nation and to Christendom. She will have to contend for the truth as it is in Jesus against various and subtle forms of error. May she do so in the strength of the Lord and in the power of his might. May she take her stand on great principles; on the sufficiency of Holy Scripture as set forth in her sixth Article, on the just authority of the Church, as a witness and keeper of Holy Writ, on the true understanding and right administration of the Sacraments, as outward signs to all of inward grace to the faithful, on justification through the sole merits of Jesus Christ by faith in his blood, on the duty of adding to faith virtue, and to virtue charity.

Yes, Christian brethren, let us contend earnestly for the faith once delivered to the saints, but let us ever remember that all our doings without charity are nothing worth. 'God is love; and he that dwelleth in love dwelleth in God, and God in him.'

Such be your happy experience, my ministerial brethren. May ye ever know that ye dwell in Him and He in you, because He hath given you of His Spirit: and in that knowledge and in that power may ye testify the truth of truths, that the Father sent the Son to be the Saviour of the world. To that blessed Trinity, Father, Son, and Holy Ghost, let us ascribe all glory and power.

SERMON XI.

THE DOCTRINE OF THE HOLY TRINITY.

BEFORE THE UNIVERSITY OF CAMBRIDGE, IN GREAT ST MARY'S CHURCH, CAMBRIDGE, ON TRINITY SUNDAY, 1872.

---

1 COR. XIII. 9, 10.

For we know in part, and we prophesy in part, but when that which is perfect is come, that which is in part shall be done away.

THE chapter cited is one which dwells in every Christian mind, and draws an echo from every loving heart. In that before it St Paul has taught his Corinthian converts to distinguish spiritual men by their several gifts of grace and their functions in the Church. At the close he says: 'seek emulously the greater gifts: and I shew you a still more excellent way.' And then, rapt with the fire of a true Christian poet, he pours forth that psalm of holy love, which fills this 13th chapter.

Love is the grace of graces. Vain, without love, is the gift of tongues, that which, in after ages, became the faculty of the Christian scholar. Vain, without love, the gift of knowledge, the faculty of the profound theologian. Vain, without love, the gift of prophecy, the faculty of the powerful preacher. 'For we know in part, and we prophesy in part, but when that which is perfect is come, that which is in part shall be done away.'

These words, if they need elucidation, are interpreted by what follows. As the human mind, when it comes to a well-instructed maturity, leaves behind and all but forgets the words, lessons, and thoughts of childhood, even so will the saint in glory forget the partial views of truth, the vague glimpses of things divine, which were a lantern to his feet while he trod the dim path of his earthly pilgrimage. 'When I was a child, I spake as a child, I thought as a child, I reasoned as a child: but since I am become a man, I have done with childish things.' Next follows in our Bible: 'Now we see through a glass darkly, but then face to face: now I know in part, but then shall I know even as also I am known.' Words which may be thus paraphrased: 'Now, in the present life, where God himself is seen of no man, we see an image of God reflected in a faulty mirror; an image, which, being indistinct to the mind's eye, is a riddle to the understanding. But then, in the future life, turned as it were towards Him, we shall see God face to face: as is the heavenly, so will they be that are heavenly: the spiritual eye will discern the Father of Spirits, in whose likeness it is born anew: will discern Him, even as itself is discerned by Him.'

Here we may ascribe to the Apostle a mental pause of awful adoration; after which, turning to his Corinthian converts again, he shows them the rank of love as highest in the triad of Christian graces. 'And now abideth faith, hope, love, these three: but the greatest of these is love.' And why? The reason lies in all that has gone before. When sight is come, faith must cease: when possession begins, hope will vanish away: but love never faileth: it goes on to infinite perfection: the foretaste of heaven here, it will be the life of heaven hereafter.

But the glory which shall be revealed is not our present theme. The text calls on us to inquire what truths and duties are suggested by St Paul, when he says to Christians generally, that they know in part, and to pastors and teachers especially, that they prophesy in part.

First then, what is it, according to St Paul, that Christian people know in part and ministers preach in part? The answer might perhaps be: all religious truth. But the 12th verse shows that what is here principally meant is the knowledge of God, of his nature and attributes; that great subject, which, in her Festival of this day, the Church authorizes and invites us to contemplate.

Standing in this place, I need scarcely say that I speak as a Churchman to Churchmen, as a believer in the doctrine of the Holy Trinity to believers in that doctrine. We believe it as a necessary deduction from the facts and statements of Scripture, and, although not formulated in a Creed during the first five or six centuries of the Church, yet virtually contained in every place where, as in the Nicene Creed and in the Te Deum laudamus, the Son and the Holy Spirit are affirmed to be co-equal with God the Father. All those amongst us, who have subscribed the confessions of the Church of England, have given our consent to this doctrine in her First Article expressly, and in her Eighth Article by implication. And if I, in all humility, rank myself with those Churchmen who would thankfully forego the liturgical use of the so-called Athanasian Creed, and in any case relieve it from its minatory clauses, this is not because I would, by the smallest tittle, weaken the recognition of the doctrine contained in it; but for two reasons: first, because that doctrine is fully recognized in the prayers and songs of our service; and prayer and song are, more properly than symbol, the constituents of common worship: secondly, because while I willingly guard the doctrine itself by the carefully drawn deductions of human reason, I am unwilling to guard any such deductions by sanction so tremendous as that expressed in the Creed 'Quicunque vult.'

Here let me ask: do we not feel that the doctrine of the Holy Trinity does in fact divide itself into two doctrines, one the oeconomic, as divines have termed it, the other the metaphysical doctrine? The first of these, which our Church teaches in her Catechism, sets forth that God, the Father of creation, is in the world, reconciling the world to Himself through Him who is God the Son, even Jesus Christ our Lord: and that God the Holy Spirit dwelleth in the hearts of the faithful, sanctifying and preparing them in his kingdom here, the Church militant, for his kingdom hereafter, the Church triumphant. This doctrine is indeed the sum and substance of Christianity. And if to be a Christian implies, as it must imply, the belief that in the name of Christ alone is salvation given, then in no other name can the Christian hope salvation for himself, or proclaim the hope of salvation to his fellow-men. Rightly therefore may he say 'Whosoever will be saved' 'must thus think of the Trinity:' yea, and to that thought he must conform his prayers, his actions, his whole life, his very self. When the marriage-feast is ready, and the servants call the guests, they that will not come, exclude themselves by their own evil choice: and they that come without the wedding garment of a pure and lively faith, shew themselves unfit to partake: *they* will be cast into outer darkness, and 'without doubt perish everlastingly' from the presence of the Lord. These are scriptural truths, from the loving lips of Jesus himself; and to publish them to mankind is not harsh denunciation, but needful and charitable warning.

The metaphysical doctrine of the Holy Trinity is situated otherwise. By this doctrine I mean the propositions framed, and by the Church received, in order to guard the correlation of Father, Son, and Holy

Spirit in the One Godhead from erroneous conception. In wording these propositions, the language of Scripture has been wisely followed as far as possible. As in the Bible, so in the Creed, the terms 'generation' and 'procession' are used in accordance with natural analogy: Filius generatur: Spiritus procedit. But where Scripture was silent, human reason stepped in to frame the terms required for definition. That in which the Divine Unity resides was called 'Substance;' better had it been 'Essence.' The term 'Person' was given to the Father, Son, and Holy Spirit, correlated in the one essence; and these are further called 'a Trinity.' The essence is not to be divided, lest any say, there be three Gods: the persons are not to be confounded, lest the Church lose the historical Christ; nor are they to be subordinated, lest the Son and the Spirit be robbed of their eternal majesty and glory. Such is the metaphysical or abstract doctrine, by which, we may shortly say, Tripersonality is confessed to be an attribute of the Divine Unity[1]. As the old dispensation said to its worshippers, 'Hear, O Israel, the Lord your God is One God;' so does the new dispensation say to its disciples: 'Hear, O Christian Israel, your One God and Lord is a Triune God.' The propositions which constitute this doctrine deal with subjects lying out of the domain of man's understanding: nay, some of them seem to contradict other conclusions, which the human intellect is

---

[1] That is, the Divine Unity comprises within itself Three CORRELATES, which theologians have, not happily, called 'Persons.'

empowered to form. We need not be startled by this admission. The reason is obvious. The conclusions of the understanding are on matter subject to the conditions of time and space. The propositions of the Creed are transcendental; they deal with the eternal, the infinite, the absolute, of which we can *know* no more than is expressed by logical negation. 'Canst thou,' says the oldest extant writing, 'canst thou find out the Almighty to perfection?' Surely not. Any revelation of the infinite to the finite must needs be partial: in other words, the doctrine of God's nature must be *expected* to be, must *be*, while man remains in his present state, a mystery, yea, the greatest of all mysteries.

'It was given,' says Augustine, 'not that it might be spoken, but that it should not remain unspoken. And what says our own Hooker? 'Although to know God be life, and joy to make mention of his name; yet our soundest knowledge is to know that we know Him not as indeed He is, neither can know Him: and our safest eloquence concerning Him is our silence, when we confess, without confession, that his glory is inexplicable, his greatness above our capacity and reach. He is above, and we upon earth; therefore it behoveth our words to be wary and few.'

By comparing the history of the doctrine itself with that of the Creed which contains it, we arrive at signal facts, suggesting important inferences. The Apostles of our blessed Lord were acquainted with the wondrous scene at his Baptism (one of them records it), with his missionary charge, with his promises as to the sending of the Holy Spirit from the Father and Himself, and with the fulfilment of those promises in their own case on the day of Pentecost: from which places, I suppose, above all others, we infer the doctrine of the Holy Trinity. And yet the nature of the Godhead seems to have been known to the Apostles in part only. So St Paul in my text avows. Certainly they prophesied in part. That 'each Person by himself is God and Lord' they have indeed amply attested; but in no genuine passage of their writings is the doctrine of the Three in One distinctly formulated. The Pauline benediction, venerable, valuable, important to the argument as it is, does not reach this character. The Church of the first three centuries, harassed by disputes on the divine nature, threatened by the errors of a Praxeas, a Noetus, a Sabellius, a Paul of Samosata, was yet enabled to defeat all these heresies without any Creed more specific than our Lord's baptismal formula. The two great Councils of the fourth century, while they condemned the false teaching of Arius and others, and established in their immortal Creed the co-eternal divinity and consubstantiality of the Son and the Holy Spirit with the Father, stopt short of the full Trinitarian definition, introducing neither the term Person, nor the word Trinity itself. The bishops at Ephesus and Chalcedon in the fifth century, occupied with disputes on the twofold nature of Christ, did not undertake to settle the larger question of the Trinity. But at some later date, we know not exactly when, we know not certainly where, we know not from whose hand, the Creed or exposition 'Quicunque vult' appeared in the Church under the manifestly spurious name of Athanasius, formulating the doctrines of the Trinity and the Incarnation in terms agreeable to the teaching of Athanasius on the former question, to the decrees of Ephesus and Chalcedon on the latter. By its keen logic this exposition obtained wide circulation as a manual of doctrine, and by its rhythmic structure it became popular as a psalm for choral use. But it is certain, I believe, (though I desire to speak under correction), that in no other community than the Church of England has it ever been *said* by the minister and congregation in divine service as a formal confession of faith. And yet the faith of the Holy Trinity is professed and firmly held by all the bodies which name the name of Christ in every land, with the exception of two or three sects, numerically small and not proselytizing. It is, therefore, not true in fact, that Trinitarian doctrine has been maintained hitherto by public recital of this Creed; and it is against reason to assert that the maintenance of that doctrine in the future depends on the retention of this Creed in the ritual of the Church of England. But whether it be retained in our Liturgy, or removed thence, it may always be subjoined to our Eighth Article among the symbols of the Church: it may stand among the fortresses which defend our Zion from the assaults of Sabellian and Socinian error.

If the great God has been pleased to grant that,

by using his gift of reason to interpret his other gift of revelation, we gain some distant and partial views of his transcendental being, let us adore with humble faith what we confess to be removed from our finite comprehension. But in the Bible, God is shewn as related to man; as our Creator, our Redeemer, our Sanctifier; and of this threefold relation there is nothing set forth, to which we may not profitably apply all the powers of the understanding, to which we may not joyfully open all the affections of the heart. St Paul indeed, in his First Chapter to the Romans, implies that even natural religion is competent to furnish that knowledge of God, which may guard men from heinous sins, if they follow its guidance heedfully. But this cannot satisfy the Christian. He looks beyond the grave. What finds he there? A moral Governor? Alas, he knows himself a sinner, having the doom of sin to dread. A bounteous Creator? That open hand sustains the race : but to the cry of the individual soul no voice replies. The Christian's hope is in the revelation of holy Scripture, and in that alone. There he finds a pardoning Father, who has given his only-begotten Son to be our Saviour; to take our flesh upon Him, to dwell amongst us, to feel and suffer with us, to die for our sins, to rise again for our justification, and to plead for us by his mediation and intercession. There he finds a life-giving Comforter, the Holy Spirit, who helpeth our infirmities, enabling us to repent, believe and love, and as regenerate and restored children to cry, Abba, Father.

Here the central figure on which the eyes of faith and hope and love repose, is the Lord Jesus Christ, 'very God and very man;' very God, who can do for us far more abundantly above all that we are able to ask or think; very man, who can speak to us with a human voice from a human heart: and with whose glorified humanity his faithful members are incorporate even here by the holy Communion of his Body and Blood. Hence it is that St Paul in all his writings sets the knowledge of Christ above all other knowledge; the knowledge of Christ, and Him crucified; the knowledge of the love of Christ which passeth knowledge. Yes, it does indeed pass knowledge. We know it only in part, we can prophesy of it only in part: but, when that which is perfect is come, if *we* are privileged to enter that blessed Kingdom, the fellowship of his saints in glory, we shall see our Saviour as He is, and know Him even as we are known.

In conclusion, let us lay to heart three great truths on the Divine Nature taught in the New Testament, with the practical duties they suggest.

God is a Spirit. Let us worship Him in spirit and in truth.

God is Light. Let us ever keep in mind that in his light only can we see light.

God is Love. Let us love Him even as He first loved us; and, by his gracious ordinance, our love will hereafter be its own immense reward, if we prove it here by the test which the Apostle of love insists on:

'Beloved, if God so loved us, we ought also to love one another.'

Note.—It has been always assumed that the Creed 'Quicunque vult' is of western authorship, because it first appeared in Spain, and in the Latin language. Is this a conclusive reason? Its manifest character of controversial subtlety seems to indicate a Greek origin. May it not have been composed in Alexandria at the close of the sixth, or beginning of the seventh century, for the settlement of the Tritheistic controversy there; and, after the Moslem conquest of Africa, have been conveyed by Christian fugitives into Spain, and translated in that country? This, it must be owned, is mere conjecture, but surely not unworthy of consideration.

SERMON XII.

CHRISTIAN MISSIONS.

PREACHED TO COUNTRY CONGREGATIONS IN THE ARCHDEACONRY OF SALOP (LICHFIELD DIOCESE) ON BEHALF OF THE SOCIETY FOR THE PROPAGATION OF THE GOSPEL, 1858—1860.

St Luke xi. 2.

Thy kingdom come.

THESE words, my brethren, are familiar to our ears, and often in our mouths. They have been repeated four times in our present service, and I trust they have made a part of our more private prayers this morning. But let me ask you, or rather, ask your own selves, this question: When you utter these words in prayer to God, do you feel their full force? Do you pray not with the lips only, but with the understanding also? not with the understanding only, but with the heart?

If you do, you must know, in the first place, that these

are very solemn words, for they are the second petition in the Lord's Prayer—that prayer which Christ himself graciously put in the mouths of his apostles, when they begged that He would teach them to pray. And the Holy Spirit has written them in the Bible for the use of Christ's people in all times; for your use and mine. Must we not then be very sure that this is one of the best petitions we can offer to our Father in heaven? that the things which it seeks must be among the best and most precious? that we ought to know and feel all that we ask for in these words? that we ought to ask for them with a fervent desire to obtain? above all, that we ought to leave nothing undone which God requires us to do on our part, in order that they may be obtained?

Let us then, in the first place, beseech God to open the eyes of our minds, that we may see what it is we ask of Him when we say 'Thy kingdom come.'

The expressions, 'kingdom of God,' and 'kingdom of heaven,' which are really one and the same, occur, as you know, very often in Holy Scripture. They may always be explained to mean either the Gospel of Christ, that is, the good tidings of salvation through Christ—the truth as it is in Jesus—or, the Church of Christ, that is, the society by which the truth as it is in Jesus is preserved, taught, and spread in the world. Now these two meanings are only various ways of saying the same thing. Just as it makes no difference whether we say, the laws require this, or, the government (if a lawful government) requires this; so it makes no difference whether we say, the Gospel requires, or, the Church (supposing it to be a true and pure Church) requires. Both the Gospel and the Church are called a kingdom, because all who embrace the Gospel and abide in the Church owe reverence and obedience to that King, who has received authority from the Father, even Christ the Lord. His subjects and servants and soldiers we are by our Christian profession. Him we are bound to worship and obey, and under his banner to fight all the days of our life.

The kingdom of God, then, is the Gospel or the Church of Christ. Now what is meant when we pray for the *coming* of that kingdom?

A kingdom is said to come when it establishes its power in any part of the world. Thus, when William the Norman conqueror came over with his army from France, his kingdom came, and established itself in this island. But no kingdom is established until it is generally obeyed. It must reign in the hearts of its subjects; they must receive and keep its laws individually, before it can be said to come in so effectual a way as to be firmly and finally established in the nation. When we pray, therefore, that God's kingdom may come, the things we really pray for are these: that the truth, as it is in Jesus, may be fully received and firmly established in our own hearts; that we may yield a willing and perfect obedience to its holy laws and precepts; in short, that Christ may reign in our hearts by faith. And not in *our* hearts only: we pray that He may reign also in the hearts of those who are near and dear to us, and of all for whom we are bound to pray; yea, in every human heart. And yet further, we desire of God in this prayer, that the Gospel and the Church of Christ may come into every corner of the earth, that it may reign every day more and more widely, more and more powerfully, more and more effectually, until all the kingdoms of the world become the kingdoms of the Lord and of his Christ; until the will of God be done by men in earth, even as it is done by the holy angels in heaven.

These are the things we pray for when we say, Thy kingdom come.

Next consider that, what Christ has taught us to pray for, He means that we should also strive for, work for, live for. An idle talking faith is no true faith at all. An idle useless Christian is no true Christian at all. Such an one is indeed in worse case than if he had never known Christ. Having the means of salvation within his knowledge and within his reach, and wilfully neglecting them, he does but increase his own condemnation. His portion will be the outer darkness of the unprofitable servant, who hid his lord's talent in a napkin, instead of putting it out to use and repaying it with interest. We must trust in God, it is true. If a farmer in our neighbourhood were to boast that his large harvests and his thriving seasons were the work of his own skill and strength alone, and were to give God none of the glory and no thanks, we should be shocked at his impiety and ingratitude; and if his fields were afterwards blighted, or his cattle smitten, we might be tempted to say, this is a judgment from heaven against him. But we must not only trust in God, we must work also. If another farmer were to stay at home all day and make long prayers, and neglect the usual work of his farm, telling us that God will give the increase of his land and stock in answer to his earnest prayers, we should say such a man was out of his mind; we should pronounce him, I fear, much more foolish than the former. And why? Because it needs great faith to feel sure that God, whom we never see, does hear and receive the prayers of his people; while we know from hard experience what is also told us in the very opening lessons of our Bible, that in the sweat of his brow man must eat his bread. It was quaintly said by the Puritan general to his troopers, 'put your trust in God, my lads, and keep your powder dry;' words which, strangely as they sound, were really the language of rational piety, as fit for the good Christian soldier who lately went to his rest, as for him who died two centuries ago; as fit for Henry Havelock as for Oliver Cromwell.

Yes, God requires us both to pray and to act, to trust and to strive: and if we do both these duties earnestly, perseveringly, faithfully, let us not doubt that all things will be made by Him to work together for our final good, though we may not always see in this life how He is bringing it to pass.

Well then: how are we to act and to strive that God's kingdom may come? How, first, that it may come in our own hearts?

'Work out your own salvation with fear and trembling,' says the Apostle, 'for it is God that worketh in you both to will and to do of his good pleasure.' How are we to work out our own salvation, God helping us by his Holy Spirit, in answer to prayer?

This is a great and fruitful, but not an easy question: and to answer it with any fulness would take a whole sermon—nay, several sermons. I must content myself now with a few heads of duty. St Paul tells you to work with fear and trembling, that is to say, with the deepest humility, knowing the weakness and sinfulness of your own hearts, and the cunning and malice of your enemy, who is ever on the watch to surprize and deceive you, ever manœuvring to make you disobey and disown Christ, and grieve the Holy Spirit, who worketh in you for good. Watchfulness therefore must go along with prayer. You must be on the alert, like good sentinels, against every surprize, and not sleep upon your post. Again, you must examine yourselves, and call your lives to a strict account day by day, and if you find any root of bitterness within, you must pluck it up, and without delay. To self-examination you must add self-denial, stedfastly refusing yourselves not only all indulgence which you know to be contrary to God's laws, but everything which seems likely to weaken your love of God, your faith in Christ, and the power of the Spirit in your soul. You must strive withal carefully and lovingly to obey God's holy will and commandments in every particular, not as relying for salvation on any works of your own, or on anything else than the sole merits of Him who died to save you, but as remembering that practice is one appointed way of strengthening and promoting faith: for he who doeth Christ's will shall know of his doctrine. Finally, you must make diligent use of all the means of grace given in the Church of Christ—the study of the holy Scriptures, which make men wise unto salvation; private prayer; devout attendance in God's house, and the Communion of your Saviour's Body and Blood. 'If ye do these things' in spirit and in truth, 'ye shall never fall: for so an entrance shall be ministered unto you abundantly into the everlasting kingdom of our Lord and Saviour Jesus Christ.' His kingdom of grace will have come to you now: and you will come to his kingdom of glory hereafter.

Next, how are we to work in order that God's kingdom may come to the world at large? Every good Christian does this in some degree, as far as his family and his neighbours are concerned, by the power of a holy example; by letting his light so shine before men, that they may see his good works, and glorify their Father which is in heaven. But this is not all that God requires of the Christian—not all He has put it in the Christian's power to do for the coming of his Master's kingdom in the world. God it is who gives you all the goods you enjoy in this life, be they large or small: you hold them from his hand, and during his pleasure; and, after providing for the wants of your families, He expects you to devote some portion of what remains to the uses of his kingdom here on earth. If thus you pray and strive that God's kingdom may come in your own hearts; if thus ye spend and be spent that God's kingdom may come in the hearts of others and in the world at large, then are you loyal subjects and servants of Christ your King, and when

He cometh the second time in his glory to judge the world, to you will be spoken those words of gladness, 'Well done, thou good and faithful servant, enter thou into the joy of thy Lord.'

Such an opportunity is afforded you now. As your friend in Christ, I beseech you in his name not to neglect it. I ask you to contribute to the funds of the Society for the Propagation of the Gospel in Foreign Parts. This Society has been established more than two centuries: for the last century and a half it has been the chief instrument in God's hand to uphold the ministration of his holy Word and Sacraments in the Colonies of the British empire: and for many years past it has taken a great share in the further, and not less momentous, work of carrying the light of Gospel truth to the heathen nations which lie in darkness and the shadow of death.. The cares and labours of this noble Society extend to almost every part of our globe. Africa, India, North America, Australia, the many isles of the two great Oceans, possess Christian ministrations by its means in great measure: its praise is in all their churches. What can I say more than this:— that while, at the beginning of this century, there were only two Bishops' Sees in all the colonies of Great Britain, there are now established as many as forty. Yes, my brethren, no fewer than forty colonial dioceses enjoy the ministry of our Church in all its fulness and beauty. This great and good work is, I repeat, mainly due to the efforts of that Society for which I now ask your liberal aid. And whence have the means to accomplish it been chiefly derived? From the voluntary gifts of the faithful; from such gifts as you may this day make. For do not, no—I intreat you—do not suppose that this work is being yet done as largely and as well as it might be done, if there were more faith and more love among those who are called Christians.

We have indeed reason to bless God and to feel great encouragement on account of the increase of this Society's income during the past year, and the fact that within the last ten years its subscriptions have been nearly doubled: but the labourers are still too few for the gathering in of the vast harvest of souls yet unconverted to the truth as it is in Jesus. How many millions of our fellow-creatures have never heard the name of Christ! How many more millions—the blinded Hindoos, for instance, worshippers of devil and monkey-gods, and the not idolatrous indeed, but equally bigoted Mahometans—whose joint treacheries and horrible cruelties to our poor dear country-people have made our hearts bleed with pity and thrill with indignation; these creatures of the same God with ourselves, whom the same Redeemer died to save, live in vast numbers within the sound of Sabbath bells, yet never bow the knee, nor lift up the voice of thanksgiving to the God and Father of our Lord Jesus Christ. Converts indeed there are among them; and far be it from us to despise the day of small things: but 180 millions remain to be converted: and who is sufficient for the work? Lord, increase our faith; Lord, enlarge our love; Lord of the vineyard, send forth more labourers into thy vineyard. India is indeed, and seems long likely to be, the greatest and most arduous field of Christian missions. Australia, New Zealand, the Cape, the North American colonies,—all give the fullest and fairest promise of becoming wholly Christianized by God's blessing within a moderate time. But in the East Indies we must go on working in faith and hope, thankful for the smallest openings and the least encouragements, which the Almighty goodness shall vouchsafe: comforted by the rich promise of Holy Writ, that the mountain of the Lord's house *shall* be established in the top of the mountains, *shall* be exalted above the hills, and all nations *shall* flow to it; and humbly acknowledging the truth of our Lord's admonition, that it is not for us to know the times and the seasons, which God hath put in his own power. 'My Father worketh hitherto, and I work,' said our blessed Saviour. And shall not we, whom He has bought with a price, even with his own blood, work too with Him in faith and hope, that his kingdom may soon come, his will be done in all the earth? Few of you, probably, are rich in this world's goods; some of you are poor, having a hard struggle for the meat that perisheth. Remember the widow's mite and the blessing which rested upon it, and ask yourselves whether you could not spare one halfpenny every week for the missionary cause. If five million British men and women would put aside one poor halfpenny every week for this noble work, we should have half a million pounds a year for the propagation of the Gospel of love. But, if you are indeed too poor to give your mite (and herein, remember, you have God not man for a witness and a judge) any of you can give your prayers; and is it not written that the effectual fervent prayer of a righteous man availeth much?

Hear one consideration more. God will not rest from this work. God will at last achieve the full coming of his kingdom. We must all be either willing helpers of this his everlasting purpose, or its unwilling tools. Choose ye this day which ye will be. When that kingdom shall come in the full blaze of its glory, when He, who once appeared as the Saviour of the world, shall appear the second time as its Judge, the unprofitable servant will be cast into outer darkness, while they who have turned many to righteousness will shine as the stars for ever and ever.

As ye are Christians, then, help this truly Christian society: as ye are Churchmen, help the Church of Christ to fulfil its King's command: 'Go and teach all nations, baptizing them in the name of the Father, and of the Son, and of the Holy Ghost:' to whom be glory now and evermore. Amen.

SERMON XIII.

THE SAFEGUARDS OF CHRISTIAN BOYHOOD.

PREACHED AT ST ANDREW'S COLLEGE, BRADFIELD, BERKS, 1860.

MARK XIV. 38.

Watch and pray, lest ye enter into temptation.

You will remember when and where and by whom these words were spoken. During those dark hours of mysterious agony, which our Redeemer passed in the garden of Gethsemane before his arrest, he had ordered his disciples to tarry apart from him and watch, that his lonely prayer might not be interrupted. After a short interval, He came again and found them sleeping, and said unto Peter, 'Simon, sleepest thou? couldest not thou watch one hour? Watch ye and pray, lest ye enter into temptation. The spirit truly is ready, but the flesh is weak.'

The text, though uttered first in these peculiar circumstances and with special reference to the temptation, which would urge Peter and the other apostles to desert their Lord in the coming season of trial, does however, most certainly, convey a warning and a command to Christians of every age and in every state and condition of mortal life : for all have the vows of Christ upon them ; all are exposed to the temptations of the world, the flesh, and the devil ; all in some unguarded hour may yield to one or other of these temptations, and refuse to bear their Master's cross.

Let us, then, now consider what is said to ourselves by these words of the Lord Jesus Christ: and be it our present exercise of watchfulness and prayer to hear with awakened hearts the message of his love, and to pray for his grace, that we may understand and accept and obey it thankfully. O Lord Jesu Christ, holy and true, Thou that openest and no man shutteth, open both the lips of the preacher, that his mouth may show forth Thy praise : and the hearts of those who hear, that they may attend unto the things that are spoken, and be faithful to Thee.

The text brings before us two duties : (1) that we watch : (2) that we pray : (3) and it likewise suggests a special motive for watching and praying, an end to be gained thereby—lest we enter into temptation.

1. And first let us consider the duty of watchfulness. Our Lord would have us 'watch.' The word in this place, and in many others, means, 'to wake up,' 'to be awake.' And as it is addressed to sleeping men, and as in St Luke we read simply, 'rise and pray,' we should hardly be justified in using this text

alone to enforce the general duty of wakefulness. Our Lord might be conceived as saying no more than this, that the hour of temptation was at hand, and it was high time to pray for deliverance from it. But we must look at this passage in connection with many others, which represent watchfulness itself as an ever urgent and never to be neglected duty, and for this reason, because we know neither the day nor the hour wherein the Son of man cometh. Such are the words with which our Lord concludes the parable of the ten Virgins. And again He says to his disciples, three days before his crucifixion, speaking of the destruction of Jerusalem, which was a type of the final destruction of the world: 'Take ye heed, watch and pray: for ye know not when the time is.' And again: 'What I say unto you, I say unto all, Watch.' So St Paul in general terms exhorts the Colossians to continue in prayer, and watch in the same with thanksgiving: while to Timothy he says, 'Watch thou in all things.'

Watchfulness, then, is a great Christian duty. How should it be otherwise? The Christian is in peril of his spiritual life daily and hourly. He is a stranger and a pilgrim upon earth, bound to a far country, which he cannot reach but through much toil and trial and tribulation. He is a soldier on the march through a hostile country, where the enemies of his soul lie in ambush at every turn to gain the vantage over him. He is a servant waiting the arrival of his lord: and his loins must be girt about and his lights burning, that, when his lord cometh and knocketh, he may open unto him immediately. In all these characters, indeed in every character the Christian can bear on this side the grave, he must watch. He must be wakeful-hearted, for he is set in the midst of temptations, some of which our Lord and his apostles notice as specially opposed to this very grace of watchfulness itself:—I mean the temptations of sloth and self-indulgence. The safeguard of watchfulness is sobriety. The evil servant who said, 'my lord delayeth his coming,' began to eat and drink with the drunken. The rich man who neglected his own soul, fared sumptuously every day, till at length he died, and found himself in torments. Our Lord warns his disciples: 'Take heed to yourselves, lest at any time your hearts be overcome with surfeiting and drunkenness.' 'Let us not sleep, as do others,' says St Paul, 'but let us watch and be sober.' And St Peter: 'The end of all things is at hand: be ye therefore sober, and watch unto prayer.'

Thus again and again does the Spirit of God call us to sobriety and watchfulness. To obey implicitly a command from God, even when we do not fully understand it, is at once our plain duty and our best interest. But oftentimes his love permits us to see clearly that his service is indeed a reasonable service. And so in this case. Foremost among the reasons which recommend watchfulness to the Christian are these two: the deceitfulness of sin and the power of habit. Sin is a subtle and delusive mischief: and even into the baptized Christian's heart, which ought to be a temple of the Holy Ghost, pure and undefiled, it seeks to enter by a thousand avenues every day and every hour: and alas! into many a heart it finds the entrance only too easy. It is like the insect, which lays its minute egg in the bud, carrying blight to the future flower and destruction to the fruit. Little sins breed great; and by a natural law, repeated sinning forms the habit of sin: while habitual sin tends to sear the conscience, and determine the wretched character of one who is sensual, not having the Spirit, outcast from God, to whom the mist of darkness is reserved for ever. Therefore to all, but to you especially, whose young minds are more plastic to the moulder's hand, we say, be sober, be vigilant. Watch against all sin. Watch against evil of every kind: against evil thoughts, which pollute the soul: against evil words, which disturb the foundations of moral principle: against evil acts, which harden the heart against good, and gradually make the reckless and the godless character. Sins may be repented of, but they cannot be annihilated. God may pardon: the soul may have faith in Christ its Saviour. But this faith has to be maintained by harder struggles against stronger foes. Every inch of ground won for holiness costs greater efforts, more scalding tears, more heart-devouring agonies. The habitual sinner, if saved he be, will be saved, as it were, by fire. ''Can the Ethiopian change his skin, or the leopard his spots? then may ye also do good, that are accustomed to do evil.'

But (2) it is Christ's command, and the will of God that we pray. There is no duty more familiar to us than this of prayer. We acknowledge it by our daily acts of devotion, public and private: we take it not only from the precepts of Christ, but from his example: not only has He commanded his followers to pray; He has taught them how to pray. Watchfulness, without prayer, were little better than presumptuous sin. Many and mighty are the adversaries of our souls, and our own strength is perfect weakness. Hold thou us up, O God, and we shall be safe. Watch indeed we must, because God will have us work out our own salvation with fear and trembling: but pray we must also, because it is God that worketh in us both to will and to do of his good pleasure: and his help is promised to prayer in his Son's name. 'Whatsoever ye ask in my name, believing,' said our Lord, 'ye shall receive.' God *can* give all that is good: for every good gift and every perfect gift cometh from above, from the Father of lights. And to the Christian, God *will* give all that is good: for 'He who spared not his own Son, but delivered him up for us all, how shall he not with him also freely give us all things?'

And (3) we are commanded to watch and pray, lest we enter into temptation. We desire of God in the Lord's prayer, 'Lead us not into temptation.' Put away from us all trials which endanger faith and virtue; for, willing as we may be in the spirit to resist and stand, the flesh is weak, and we *may* fall. 'But deliver us from evil.' But if we do come into temptation, as needs we often must in this frail mortal state, if faith and virtue *are* dangerously tried, then do Thou, O Lord, deliver us. 'What time I am afraid, I will trust in thee. In God have I put my trust, I will not fear what flesh can do unto me.' 'Yea, though I walk through the valley of the shadow of death, I will fear no evil, for thou art with me: thy rod and thy staff, they comfort me.'

The temptations to which the baptized Christian is exposed are set forth in our Church Catechism under three well-known heads: those of the world, the flesh, and the devil. These are what we have all promised in Baptism, and most of us in Confirmation, to renounce. Now the temptations of the flesh are those which enter by way of the senses, inviting to unlawful or immoderate indulgence; to all that is impure in thought, word or deed: to drunkenness, gluttony, sloth: to all excess of even those pleasures which are wholesome when moderately enjoyed. The temptations of the devil (though that fallen spirit is the agent of all temptation) are more especially those which caused his fall, those which incite us to sin against truth, justice, reverence, charity; those which tend to make us liars, robbers, blasphemers, slanderers, murderers; the sins of falsehood, pride, envy, wrath, revenge. The temptations of the world are all those which lead us to prefer the favour or the fear of our fellow-creatures to the favour and the fear of our Creator: the society of earthly friends to communion with the Father of Spirits, a hollow peace with men to the peace of God in the heart. These temptations are countless, endless. Their name is legion. And they are of all the subtlest and the most dangerous: for these are the temptations whose power for evil is widest and strongest and most dominant in the tone-giving classes of mankind: these are the temptations, which worked upon a Judas to betray his Master, upon a Pilate to crucify the guiltless Jesus. These, young Christians, await your entrance on the stage of life, to beguile you with their blandishments, or to appal you with their threats; these will entice you, like Peter, to deny the Lord who bought you; to refuse the burden and the reproach of the cross; yea, even to fall away from your heavenly gift, and, following the fashions of a corrupt world, to crucify to yourselves the Son of God afresh, and put him to an open shame. While you watch and pray against all temptation, against the temptations of youthful lusts, against the temptations of devilish passions, guard most carefully, pray most earnestly against the low standards, the specious sophistries, the corrupting opinions of a world that lieth in wickedness. The friendship of this world is enmity against God.

You are placed for a while aloof from these temptations, that by God's help you may be trained and strengthened against the time when you will have to confront them. You are placed aloof from that world which calls itself the great, so narrow and poor in the eyes of one who seeks a better country, that is, an heavenly. Needs must I regard you, students of this lovely rural Academe, with more than even the Christian's ordinary sympathy, for I have a personal interest in your well-being; and over you, watching for your souls as they that must give account, are men over whom in past days I also have watched under the same awful obligation. I pray God and the Father of our Lord Jesus Christ that you may be enabled to use aright the opportunities of good which are here within your reach. Though far, as yet, from that wider world I spoke of, you live in a little schoolboy world, which has trials and temptations of its own, trials and temptations against which you have to watch and pray. With all the good which God vouchsafes, there comes to us fallen creatures a temptation to neglect or to abuse it: and good neglected or abused is evil, is sin. Think of this when you come to your daily devotions in this house of prayer: remember that God is a Spirit, and they that worship Him must worship Him in spirit and in truth. Languid devotion, lip-worship, prayers uttered without an uplifted heart, or choked by idle thoughts, these are sin. Your public worship needs to be guarded and supported by your private devotions. Watch and pray against all such temptations. Pray every morning that you may have grace and strength to pray. Examine yourselves every evening whether you have prayed with the heart and with the understanding. And when your conscience condemns you, repent of this sin among others, and desire with earnest prayer God's pardon for the past and God's help for the future. Watchfulness, self-examination, prayer, these are the daily exercises of a Christian soldier; these, with the careful study of God's word, are a discipline training him to fight the good fight of faith, that in the end he may more than conquer through Him that loved him.

There is yet another temptation to which I can imagine that some of you may be exposed. Perhaps you regret that this training-place of your boyhood, however beautiful and well-appointed, is not among the ancient and long-renowned foundations of your country. Against this feeling you should watch and pray; for, although natural, it is neither just nor wise. Every earthly thing which we now call old, was once new: and social change and social growth demand the continual evolution of the new, and the continual renovation of the old. That which decayeth and waxeth old, says the Apostle to the Hebrews concerning the Mosaic covenant, is ready to vanish away. I thought of this text when, some short time since, I stood on the palace of the Senators. I looked eastward over the widespread ruins of imperial Rome. It decayed, it waxed old (I said), it was worn out : it has long since vanished away. I looked westward to the Vatican—the seat of Papal rule, and again I said : it decays, it waxes old, it is wearing out, it is ready to vanish away. No, my young friends, misjudge not the new : do we not look for new heavens and a new earth, wherein dwelleth righteousness? Rather let the consideration that you are members of a new school inspire you to win wreaths of honour for that school by the fruitfulness of your studies here ; by your virtuous emulation, by your successful industry, by your moral and intellectual worth as Christian scholars and gentlemen : by the purity of your conduct, by the usefulness of your lives.

The school to which I belonged had not yet been

open for three years to the youth of the realm, when it numbered among its scholars two who were destined to live for ever in the bright roll of England's clerisy and chivalry, knights and patriots, scholars and poets— Philip Sidney, and Fulke Greville. Glad should I be to think that I now see before me the Sidneys and the Grevilles of St Andrew's College, those to whom future inmates of these classic shades may look back through long years as household names, types of excellence, patterns for imitation. Yet why do I speak of Sidneys and of Grevilles, erring men, however great, when you are privileged to lift up your eyes to the model of perfection, the Lord of glory, Jesus Christ the righteous, who gave Himself not only to die for your sins, but also to live as your example? Him set before your eyes, a standard ever to be approached, never to be attained. Watch and pray, study and strive, that the same mind be in you, which was also in Him. Count all things loss for the excellency of the knowledge of Christ Jesus your Lord. Press toward the goal for the prize of the high calling of God in Him. Walk neither now nor in years to come with the enemies of the Cross of Christ, who mind earthly things; but while yet on earth live as citizens of heaven, looking for your Lord's second coming, that ye may be found of Him in peace without spot, blameless.

SERMON XIV.

BEFORE THE UNIVERSITY OF CAMBRIDGE.

THE COMMEMORATION OF BENEFACTORS, BEING THE SERMON OF THE LADY MARGARET'S PREACHER FOR 1873.

---

2 PETER III. 8.

But, beloved, be not ignorant of this one thing, that one day is with the Lord as a thousand years, and a thousand years as one day.

WERE my text adduced in support of some difficult or disputed doctrine, I should probably refrain from citing an Epistle of questionable authenticity. But these words are the vivid expression of a truth apparent in all the teaching of Holy Writ, a truth implied in our conception of the Divine nature, as free from the limitation of time as well as space. They are an evident reminiscence of that grand Psalm, which Jewish tradition has entitled a Prayer of Moses the man of God.

"Lord, thou hast been our dwelling-place in all generations: thou turnest man to destruction, and sayest, 'Return, ye children of men.' For a thousand years in thy sight are but as yesterday when it is past, and as a watch in the night."

Not merely as a beautiful speculation does either Hebrew Psalmist or Christian Apostle set forth this doctrine of God's unchangeable and illimitable nature. They make it 'profitable for reproof, for correction, for instruction in righteousness.' The Psalmist, while he contrasts the timeless Creator with the time-bound creature, the One who is from everlasting to everlasting with the many whose years are threescore and ten, yet shews to us the Eternal as a God who heareth prayer; who, if we open our ears to him, will teach us so to number our days that we may apply our hearts unto wisdom; will satisfy us with his mercy, when we penitently call upon him; and establish the work of our hands upon us, when it is done according to his holy laws. And it is the yet happier privilege of the Christian teacher to exhibit the Father of our Lord Jesus Christ as a covenanted God, who is not slack concerning his promise, as some men count slackness, but is preparing new heavens and a new earth, wherein dwelleth righteousness, for all who in this life of trial have faithfully striven to grow in grace, and in the knowledge of their Lord and Saviour Jesus Christ. Thus does my text, read in connexion with its context, bring before us, on the authority of both covenants, our individual duty in this life; to apply our hearts unto godly wisdom by study and meditation and holy living, with prayer; that so by the Spirit's aid we may work out our own salvation, and finally come into God's presence through the mediation of his blessed Son.

But the special service of this morning carries our thoughts for a while beyond the sphere of individual duty.

If time has been rightly defined to be the order of succession, then we must say that with creation time came in. The phrase of Moses and St John—'In the beginning'—refers us back to the origin of time, when God made lights to be for signs and for seasons, and for days and years: 'My Father worketh hitherto, and I work,' said our Divine-human Pattern; and on his authority we are entitled to say, that the Creator himself gave to the creature made in his image the law and the example of work. Happy they who in this life are labourers together with God: for they shall enter into his rest.

Although the Finite may never hope to comprehend the Infinite, yet as the smallest asteroid in our planetary system draws its speck of light from the vast solar reservoir, even so may the contemplation of God's timeless nature supply valuable lessons for the improvement of time.

Passing by that trite theme of poet and moralist, the rebuke which my text addresses to the boast of heraldry, the pride of long descent, whether from Saxon thane or Norman cavalier, let us consider more attentively the corrective it applies to one of the most potent and natural feelings of the human mind, the feeling, I mean, which ascribes to long possession and prescription an indefeasible right. Surely there is much, very much, to be said in defence of this principle. And yet upon the history, rather may we say upon the histories, of that great Aryan race, which leads the march of human civilization, there is written a law of change—change not always from the worse to the better, but oftentimes from seeming good to manifest evil—yet shewn upon the whole to be a law of progress, a law which may be justly ascribed to that supreme Legislator with whom one day is as a thousand years, and a thousand years as one day.

Eighteen years before the Christian era, the great lyric poet of the Augustan age challenged for his songs an immortal popularity in words to this effect:

> 'I shall not wholly die : still fresh shall bloom
> my future praise, while with the silent virgin
> the Pontiff shall ascend the Capitol.'

Still fresh, after nineteen centuries, blooms the praise of Horace. But when just four centuries had elapsed from the date of that ode, the Pontiff with the silent virgin ceased to ascend the Capitol. The youthful Gratian, reared in a purer faith, had scornfully refused those splendours of the chief Pontificate which a long line of Roman emperors had been proud to accept: the Vestal Virgins, shorn of their dignity, stript of their revenues, were left to penury, while the virtuous and accomplished Symmachus in vain deprecated that suppression of the ancient rites, which, demanded by the voice of Ambrose, was finally sanctioned by the decrees of Theodosius. Then, like a lamp easily blown out, expired from the world that brilliant ritual of Greece and Rome, which had lasted historically more than ten centuries, traditionally more than twenty. The hour of its doom had struck at last: for one day is with the Lord as a thousand years, and a thousand years as one day.

When Symmachus would fain have sheltered decaying polytheism from the stroke of despotic power allied to Christian intolerance (for to tolerate idols was indeed to deny Christ), he naturally pleaded the cause of old prescription against innovating change, and asserted the sanctity of endowments against the threatened violation of testamentary gifts. Who, it was then urged, would hereafter be willing to bestow or bequeath for the service of religion, if his bounty, instead of being preserved to its destined uses, were even turned against them by the reckless hand of invading power? His rhetoric did not convince: his prophecies were not fulfilled. We all know how largely the treasures of the faithful were poured into the lap of the Latin Church, what lands were enfeoffed to it, what provinces were yielded to its sway; how the fabulous donation of Constantine was more than realized by the lavish gratitude of the Carlovingian kings and emperors.

The limits of this discourse forbid me to dwell on the many great and good uses to which the increasing wealth of the Church was applied, or on the numerous abuses by which, alas, it was too often desecrated. Many of us have lately celebrated one of the happiest instances, one in which the devotion of large wealth to religious use has produced good almost without alloy. I speak of the foundation of the Abbey of Ely twelve centuries ago by the pious Saxon princess Etheldreda. Out of that donation grew in after years the see of Ely, with its splendid cathedral: a see filled from age to age by many learned and excellent prelates, by none more excellent than him, who, regretted by all the clergy and laity of his diocese, now leaves it for another sphere of duty, in which we pray that the God and Saviour, whose faithful servant he is, may be with him and bless him still, and prosper his work upon him. Nor should we in Cambridge omit to recognise our own special debt of gratitude to Etheldreda's gift, since it enabled two Bishops of Ely to plant Colleges in this University, one, our oldest collegiate foundation, dating from the thirteenth century, the other from the close of the fifteenth.

When we hear to-day the long roll of our benefactors, Christian men and women, who, in the words of the Son of Sirach, 'have left a name behind them, that their praises might be reported,' extending from that East Anglian prince, who is said to have lit a taper of learning here in the seventh century, to those honoured worthies of the northern shires, the Whewells and Sedgwicks, who have gone to their rest within the last few years, we perceive how strongly in every age the Christian mind has grasped that great truth which St Paul ascribed to our Lord's own lips, 'it is more blessed to give than to receive:' how cheerfully it has appropriated those lessons of the Hebrew Preacher (Ecclesiastes, Ch. XI.) which are indeed a scriptural 'locus classicus' on the motives and rules of beneficence. 'Cast thy bread upon the waters,' thy rice-seed, that is, on the flooded land: 'for thou shalt find it after many days.' The seed of bounty which thou sowest in the world shall, by God's blessing, be fruitful and bring forth, some thirty, some sixty, some an hundred-fold. And thou shalt find it after many days. yea, thou thyself shalt find it: for is it not written, 'whatsoever a man soweth, that shall he reap'? if not in this life, yet in the world of spirits. 'Give a portion to seven and also to eight.' Stint not thy bounty to a few, if thou canst diffuse it more widely: 'for thou knowest not what evil shall be upon the earth.' Thou knowest not what may befall in the changes of human life: what evil may be averted or alleviated by thy bounty, by its example, if not by its operation. 'If the clouds be full of rain, they empty themselves on the earth.' God is rich in goodness: He sendeth his rain upon the just and upon the unjust. Be thou perfect, even as thy Father which is in heaven is perfect. 'He that observeth the wind shall not sow, and he that regardeth the clouds shall not reap.' Whoso scans with too nice distrust the occasions of doing good is likely to do no good to others, and to lose for himself the great good of doing good. 'In the morning sow thy seed, and in the evening withhold not thine hand: for thou knowest not whether shall prosper, either this or that, or whether they both shall be alike good.' Lose no opportunity of doing good: and leave the issues of thy bounty to Him, who is the author and giver of all good.

Such lessons of love and piety most of our benefactors had probably learnt. The princely lady, whose preacher I am this day, had certainly learnt them in the school of trial and sorrow. Whatever were the miseries of the times in which the Hebrew Preacher wrote, miseries which wrung from his heart that αἴλινον αἴλινον, that sorrowful burden of the vanity of all things human, they could hardly have been sadder than the scenes witnessed by the Lady Margaret of Richmond during the years of youth and middle life. Herself the rich heiress of a Beaufort, akin to the reigning house of Lancaster, daughter-in-law, by her first marriage, to the royal widow of the hero of Azincourt, she was so far exceptionally fortunate, that, although thrice wedded, she lost no husband by the sword or the axe. But as maid and matron she witnessed the horrors of the bloodiest civil war that ever desolated this island. She saw battles, like that of Towton, more wasteful of human life than the Moskwas and Gravelottes of modern warfare. She saw the nobility and gentry of England more than decimated on the battlefield and the scaffold. Her own numerous kinsmen, Beauforts, Staffords, Tudors, died, like their prince, probably like their king, by a death of violence. Herself at length attainted, she was saved from further peril by the victory of her son, the seventh Henry, through whose entire reign she lived, spared to see the extinction of civil discord by the accession of her grandson, the undoubted heir of York, and acknowledged representative of the Lancastrian claim. We know from sure evidence that this illustrious lady was one who feared God and did good to men. These principles had upheld her in trial, and in her prosperous days she did not depart from them. Her wise piety was shewn in choosing for her confessor and executor the learned and upright Fisher, who, preaching her funeral sermon, summed up his testimony with these words: 'She had in a manner all that is praisable in a woman, either in soul or body.'

Some will say that, when the Lady Margaret gave one portion of her wealth to found Readerships in Divinity within both Universities, with a Preachership in Cambridge, a second portion to found a College here, dedicated to her Redeemer Christ, a third to endow a still larger College, bearing the name of his Beloved Disciple, St John, she was a member of the Anglican Church as it then stood, in communion with the Church of Rome, and obedient to the Pope. They will say, that, had she lived to witness the severance of that communion, she would have viewed this event as an evil upon the earth; she would have deemed it a deadly sin to promote the doctrines of the Reformation by founding institutions to teach them. And such statement they might confirm by recalling the brave integrity of her counsellor and confessor Bishop Fisher, who refused at the cost of his own life to abjure the Papal supremacy. Man cannot determine the persistence of an untried faith. God alone knows whether the Lady Margaret, like her descendants the Marys, would have walked still in the old paths, or like her descendant Elizabeth, would have chosen the path which we deem to be older still as well as truer. We may grant that the former is the more probable alternative: nor need we either disparage the virtue of those who died honestly for the papal cause, or palliate the sin of any who promoted change for selfish ends. In the result we thankfully discern the working of that providence which overruled evil for good. And, as regards the Christian bounty of all our benefactors who lived and died before the Reformation, we say that what they gave could be given and received only in subordination to the principles of human progress. The first donors adapted their gifts to the wants and occasions of their own age, knowing not what evil should be upon the earth. Another generation, having experienced much evil, applies that experience to modify the former benefaction; and so on to the end of time. We do not say that all change is equally wise, just, and happy: and for those who promote and conduct change, grave indeed and responsible is the duty of seeing that it be wisely, justly, and happily made. But from the general law of progress there is no escape: sometimes with slower, sometimes with swifter motion, the stream of human history flows onward to its unseen issue, under the supreme direction of an all-wise and almighty Will.

The Lady Margaret of Richmond knew no cult but that of Rome. Therein the pious lady found peace and hope, and, we doubt not, the salvation of her soul. Free thought had indeed striven to assert itself here and there at various times; but had striven in vain. Abelard had been condemned, imprisoned, silenced. The Puritans of Southern France had been extirpated by fire and sword; the Vaudois driven, like wild beasts, into their mountain lairs. The Utraquist of Bohemia, the Lollard of England, with the bones of his teacher Wicliffe, had been given to the flames. The structure of the Gregories and the Innocents seemed to be impregnable. Yet the Lady Margaret had not lain in her grave ten years, ere free thought again burst its barriers, and this time to be trodden out no more, this time to wage a more successful struggle against the power and influence of Rome, against Rome's imperial and royal allies, against the craft of the Jesuit, the fires of the Inquisition, and the dagger of the fanatic. In the seething whirlpool of religious wars and persecutions did Europe writhe for two centuries and a half, until the weary combatants suddenly found themselves in the presence of common foes, new and terrible—philosophic infidelity and popular insurrection.

And to us, who are drawing nigh to the last quarter of the nineteenth century, what is the outcome of this turmoil? Whither is His hand guiding us, with whom one day is as a thousand years, and a thousand years as one day?

Do I err in believing that one phase of the coming future, one step in the divinely-guided progress of the human race, will be the common consent of Christian nations to establish and maintain liberty of conscience in religion?

We, brethren, in this illustrious University, have a large liberty of studies, established by the wise and progressive energies of our own academic body. We have a large liberty, some may think it too large, of using or neglecting these advantages. We are throwing out our tentacles ever more and more for the advancement of science and learning. Our local examinations have been the means of stimulating with good effect the higher education of both sexes in this land: and our teaching power is now eagerly sought by the great centres of industry in our northern and midland counties. Finally, after long discussion and dispute, our rulers have annexed liberty of conscience to our degrees and to most of our endowments, academic and collegiate. These measures of the Legislature I do not cite for the purpose of either praise or blame: 'the wisest witnesses' says a Greek poet, 'are the days to come.' I cite them as facts merely; and I ask you, my brethren, (yet why need I *ask* you to do what all alike recognize as a sacred duty?) to use them, as far as they can be used, for the glory of God and the promotion of Christian truth.

Be it remembered that, along with liberty of conscience we have its inseparable adjunct, liberty of association. Hereafter, every lay member of this University will be a Christless man, if he does not join his personal unit of example and encouragement to that which he deems to be the purest and best cult in Christ's Church now on earth.

Here, we doubt not, as in every large centre of population, the choice will be a wide one. Here will be found (though its worshippers, we are warned, will be few, if any) the cult of Rome, with which most of us are familiar from booklore and from continental travel. Here will be found the cult of those who call themselves Anglo-catholics, leaning to ritual and æsthetic embellishment; and, though confined by law to the language and order of the English liturgy, yet emulating the Roman cult in its endeavour to display symbolically the dignity and power of the priestly office, the real presence of the Saviour in the Eucharist, and the grace of the Holy Spirit in Baptism. Here will be found the cult of the simpler Churchman, who, studious of peace and comprehension as well as of decent order and cheerful godliness, is content to commemorate his Lord's death and passion as the Lord himself ordained, trusting his gracious promise that, wherever two or three are assembled in his Name, there is He in the midst of them. Here too will be found the various cults of nonconformity, with which I am not familiar, but which agree with our own, I suppose, in worshipping, generally, one Father, one Redeemer, one Spirit, three in one God.

Hereupon two questions may arise:

First: will not liberty of conscience bring into our body those to whom all varieties of cult are alike indifferent, an irreligious class? The answer is given from personal experience. Tests excluded from our degrees the religious dissenter; but they did not in general keep out unbelievers, who, having joined no other communion, deemed it morally allowable to profess themselves of the Church by law established.

A second question naturally presses itself on every thoughtful mind. If the severance of the English Church from the State, which so many combined forces are at work to achieve, should ultimately be accomplished, how will it then fare with the theological faculties in both Universities, how with their religious teaching and worship, academic and collegiate? This question I cannot answer: and I shall make no attempt to answer it. But to those who may by possibility live to witness an event which will wring from many a woeful heart the cry of αὐτίκα τεθναίην, I would utter in my concluding words an old man's earnest warning.

Common worship implies common dogma. This I fully grant. The object and conditions of worship, with the subject matter of prayer, must be settled by the common consent of those who would worship in common. But, this being done, and allowing also that the formal recital of dogma is essential to articles of faith and to catechetic instruction, whether it is likewise essential to public worship is a very questionable point. But, leaving this topic (for I have no desire to prove that our venerable Church has practically erred), I speak only of the novel cult introduced of late years into many parish churches. Let all that is beautiful in nature, let all that is noble and dignified in art enhance the public worship of God : this I gainsay not. Let all due solemnity attend that great act of worship, the Sacrament of the Lord's Supper, commemorative as it is of our Saviour's atoning love, and expressive alike of God's pardon and grace to man, and of man's lowliest penitence and most fervent gratitude to God. This too I gainsay not. But, if doctrines are to be forced on the mind through the eye, which enlightened Churchmen, who would worship God in spirit and in truth, are neither bound nor prepared to receive; if prayers and lessons are slurred with unseemly haste, and the stress of the service laid on music and ceremonial and a theurgic rite celebrated in imitation of the Roman Mass, and in opposition to the meaning of the English rubric,—then indeed I tremble for the future, then I sadly doubt whether the

Legislature will long be willing to continue the establishment of a Church so minded.

My heart's desire and prayer for our national Zion is, that it may endure and flourish and enlarge its borders: and I look on its removal as the heaviest blow which could be dealt to true religious liberty.

May God avert this evil, or if He see fit to inflict it, may He (as He surely will) overrule it for greater ultimate good.

In every case, may this our noble University be continually sustained and fed, for a beacon of light and love to the nation, by Him who is Light and Love, with whom one day is as a thousand years, and a thousand years as one day! Ἀμήν.*

---

* I have retained this Greek Amen, because it was appended by my dear friend, the late Professor Selwyn, when he borrowed this sermon for reperusal. He also wrote on the outer leaf the word 'Imprimatur,' thus endorsing the sentiments contained in it.

SERMON XV.

ON THE DEATH OF HIS ROYAL HIGHNESS THE PRINCE CONSORT, PREACHED IN ST MARY'S CHURCH, SHREWSBURY, DECEMBER, 1861.

ISAIAH XXVI. 9.

When thy judgments are in the earth, the inhabitants of the world will learn righteousness.

BRETHREN, your coming here to-day is a profession of faith. It says for you that you profess to believe in God, the Maker, Governor, and Judge of the world—in God, who speaks to you by the inward voice of conscience, by the outward acts of his power, by those writings which you revere as his word, by that Church which you own for a witness and keeper of the truth. These are not all the great things which by coming here you profess to believe; but they are those things which it concerns me to mention now, when as a minister of the Church, opening the Word, appealing to your hearts, in the name of Him who governs and judges and will judge the world, I ask you to learn and lay to heart those lessons of righteousness which his startling dispensations, called in my text the judgments of God, are fitted, and, we humbly believe, designed, to teach.

When I call some of God's dispensations startling, 'I speak,' to borrow St Paul's language, 'as a fool;' I speak, that is, in condescension to the habitual notions of erring men. If we thought more of God, if we conversed with Him more in prayer and meditation, if He were ever present to our minds as ordering all events, not those alone which recur by known laws, as day and night, months and years, but those also which surpass our calculation, as the issues of life and death, and all that we vaguely and faithlessly term casual; if, in short, we were more believing, more heavenly-minded, we should not be startled by any of the divine dispensations. And why not? Because we should be ever living with girded loins and lights burning, ever on the look out for that last and greatest of all dispensations, which will come to unprepared souls as a thief in the night— even the second coming of our Lord and Saviour Jesus Christ to judge the world.

But few, alas, are those happy servants who thus truly watch for their Lord's coming. Multitudes there are, on the other hand, who never bow the knee to God, nor lift the heart in prayer; multitudes again who say in their hearts—my Lord delayeth His coming, let us eat and drink and be merry; or, let us lay field to field. For such as these it is well when the judgments of God are in the earth, if peradventure they may be driven to learn righteousness. It is well when loss or sorrow or sickness awakens individual men from the sleep of sin to penitence and holiness. It is well when great calamities or perils arouse nations from self-complacent ease, and bring them before the mercy-seat crying, Lord, save us, we perish: Lord, we believe, help Thou our unbelief: Lord, we repent; hear Thou in heaven Thy dwelling-place, and when thou hearest, forgive.

Within the last few years, how often have public events appealed to our deepest sympathies, and claimed our earnest prayers and intercessions! And how graciously has God dealt with us through this time; how often has He allayed our anxious fears, revived our hopes, crowned our desires, and given us the oil of joy for mourning! The toils and trials and privations of our brave soldiers in the Crimean war, how painfully did we feel them! But they resulted in a splendid victory and a solid peace. The bloody massacres of the Indian mutiny—the frightful sufferings and perils of our dear country-people there—with what anguish and terror did they thrill us day after day, week after week, month after month, until the favour of God crowned our arms with success, and grief and fear were forgotten in the reconquest and reconstitution of our Eastern Empire! Have we not ample reason 'to praise the Lord for His goodness, and to declare the wonders that He doeth for the children of men'? It was our turn then from a neutral watchtower to observe the struggle of two great European nations in the plains of Lombardy—to mark the ancient power of the Papacy crumbling—to see the ideal of an Italian kingdom all but realised, and hear the triumphal shout of freedom and unity pealing around the bonfires of Etna and Vesuvius. But the growing military and naval strength of a great neighbour was not observed without a shade of fear and doubt: fear of possible aggression, doubt of our own means of internal defence. The fear might be groundless; we trust it was so: the doubt was not unfounded; and from it sprung that noble movement, whereby one hundred thousand brave right hands and loyal hearts, some of which are here present, armed and pledged themselves to the defence of their country and their Queen in the hour of need.

That hour—is it drawing nigh, or yet far distant? At this moment, we doubt not, west-winds are speeding to us across the Atlantic an answer to this question, a message of peace or war—of peace, for which let us offer our most fervent prayers to the God of peace; or of war, in which, if it comes, let us see that our quarrel be just, and humbly commend our arms to the favour of Him who has hitherto mercifully given us victory.*

But, O Father in Heaven, maker and governor of the world, how truly hast Thou told us that thy judgments are unsearchable, and thy ways past finding out! While our eyes were bent to a foreign and distant coast, awaiting thence the tidings of good or evil which thy Providence should assign, lo, suddenly, where we least looked for it, where we most felt it, thy chastening hand was raised to smite us at home. The husband and

---

* The just claim of the English Government was, happily, recognized by the President of the United States.

counsellor of our Queen, the father of our princes, the pattern of every royal virtue, he who had led all our peaceful improvements, while he wisely shunned the battle-ground of politics, this great and good man is carried to the tomb, in the vigour of his manhood, in the ripeness of his intellect, when England had learned to understand and value him, when a long career of glorious usefulness seemed to lie before him. Alas for the vanity of human hopes and wishes! 'The race is not to the swift, nor the battle to the strong; there is one event to the righteous and to the wicked; man goeth to his long home, and the mourners go about the streets; the dust shall return to the earth as it was, and the spirit shall return unto God who gave it.' Truly saith the Preacher, 'man knoweth not his time.'

Brethren, at this afflicting moment our hearts are in the house of mourning; our sympathies are with our bereaved and beloved Queen; our prayers ascend for her and hers to the throne of grace. May He, who dealt the stroke, assuage the anguish and heal the wound! May He give her strength of body and mind to rise to the full height of her arduous duties! May He nerve her to perform alone the mighty task which she had so long shared with a partner worthy of her own highly gifted nature! May He ever raise up for her wise and impartial and disinterested counsellors, fearing God, and justly entitled to the confidence of their Queen and country! Above all, may His blessing rest upon the head of her eldest son, upon that young prince, the expectancy of the state, who is now treading the threshold of manhood and public life, without a father's eye to watch his progress, a father's hand to guide his steps, a father's voice of experienced warning and encouragement in the season when his choice is to be made between the flowery and the thorny path, a choice how difficult for him, how momentous to our country! O God, our Saviour, be Thou the father of the fatherless, and a husband to the widow.

And now, brethren, recollect my opening words. You believe in a God who governs the world. You believe in Him as revealed in his holy Word. You believe, then, what that Word tells you, that his judgments are shown in the earth, and that they are shown for this purpose, amongst others, that men may learn righteousness. Do I then err, in regarding the heavy calamity which has befallen this nation in the death of the Prince Consort, as a judgment of this importance? Surely not. Its suddenness, its afflictiveness, the preciousness of what we have lost, the irreparable void left in the royal house and the national counsels, combine to mark this sad event as a signal dispensation of Providence, from which the inhabitants of the world generally, and the British people in particular, should learn righteousness.

Bowing our hearts beneath the rod of our heavenly Teacher, and humbly desiring his grace to help us, let us try to learn his lessons, and apply them to our own improvement.

The thoughts and the doctrines which link themselves with death, with sudden and premature death, with the death of the mighty of this world, suitable as they are to this Advent season, I ask you to ponder in your closets, and interweave with your prayers. I pass them by for lack of time only, not because I deem them too familiar to our minds. The disposition to ignore solemn subjects as trite, and to sneer away great truths as truisms, is one of the fatallest symptoms of our fallen and depraved nature. Happy the intellect and the heart which do not revolt from every-day nourishment. Happy they who never lose their relish for rising and setting suns and streams and flowers and birds, and the Bible and the Prayer book, and thoughts of heaven, and communion of the soul with God and Christ. Happy they: for they are fostering in the light and breath of the Holy Spirit that pure heart, which alone is privileged to see God. I ask you to consider this heavy judgment as reading to us a lesson of national righteousness. Our heavenly Father, we know, has been very gracious and merciful to us as a people. He has made us the most widely powerful, the wealthiest, and the most influential nation—all things considered—upon his earth. From the horrors of foreign invasion, which all other countries have had to endure, England has been exempt from the date of the Norman conquest. Civil war, for the last two centuries, has been rare and limited, and of brief duration. And then, brethren, during the last twenty years we have had a blessing from God for which it has behoved us to be very thankful. We have had for our Queen a virtuous woman, whose 'price is far above rubies,' and for our

Queen's husband a wise and upright and accomplished Prince, 'known in the gates when he sat among the elders of the land.' We have seen a large and thriving family of well-trained children rise up around them and call them blessed. Have they not been 'as the stones of a crown, lifted up as an ensign upon the land'? Happy England, had all its matrons been such as Queen Victoria, its husbands and fathers emulous of Prince Albert's virtues, its hearths as pure, its homes as peaceable, as the stately halls of Windsor!

But let us put the question to ourselves. Has our gratitude to our heavenly Benefactor been suitable to these his signal benefits? Has our growth in faith and holiness as a nation been in proportion to the advantages we have enjoyed? Have we habitually offered the sacrifices of righteousness, and put our trust in the Lord? Admitting considerable moral progress in some departments, as in criminal laws, prison discipline, poor laws, and popular instruction, admitting the improvements which have taken place in the parochial ministrations of our Church, and the larger help given to us by the laity—admitting frequent munificence, and some examples of heroic self-devotion in our highest and wealthiest of both sexes—admitting that our soldiers and sailors of every class and rank are unsurpassed in courage, endurance, and loyal ardour—admitting, as I do, these things, rejoicing to admit them, and being, I trust, deeply thankful for them—I fear, nevertheless, that we are far from being as truly great (by which I mean as truly good) a people as we ought to be. I fear that our standards of excellence, public, private, and professional, are lamentably low—that we treat success as the test of merit—wealth or worldly favour as the measure of success; that our education is not as deep as it is wide ; that our popular writing is not as wise and honest as it is clever and assuming; and that public opinion is in a great degree swayed by those whose rule is not truth and justice, nor their end the good of society and the glory of God. Hence, among other consequences, arises our inability to correct many crying evils, and to effect salutary changes in various departments which greatly need them. These are but a small sample of the mischiefs which lie upon and beneath the surface of society in our native land. But I would rather understate the case than appear to aggravate it. Enough for me to lay down the proposition that our moral and religious character as a nation is far from reaching the standard of God's Holy Word, far from answering duly to the benefits and advantages for which He has made us responsible.

If we grant this, and surely nothing but the blindest self-esteem will refuse to grant it, what should be our next admission? To believe in God, the judge of the world, is, as we have seen, to believe that the calamities which befall nations are judgments of God, adapted and designed to teach righteousness, either to the nation which suffers them, or in the more terrible instances—as those of Sodom and Gomorrah—to the world at large. What other lesson is taught by God's dealing with the Jews of old, by His judgments upon

Tyre, upon Babylon, upon Rome, by the whole tenor of world-history? What other lesson do we read in those chapters of the prophet Isaiah, which the church opens to us in these weeks of Advent? What other has sounded in our ears this day? 'Woe to the rebellious children,' saith the Lord, 'that take counsel, but not of me; and that cover with a covering, but not of my Spirit, that they may add sin to sin: which say to the seers, See not; and to the prophets, Prophesy not unto us right things, speak unto us smooth things, prophesy deceits. For thus saith the Lord God, the Holy One of Israel: In returning and rest shall ye be saved; in quietness and confidence shall be your strength: and ye would not. Therefore shall ye be left as a beacon on the top of a mountain, and as an ensign on a hill.'

Hear then the conclusion of the whole matter. Let us humbly acknowledge this afflictive dispensation of Almighty God as a judgment in the earth, and use it, nationally and individually, as a lesson of righteousness. Let us think more of God's great mercies, let us thank Him more heartily; let us pray more fervently that He will continue and multiply them upon us; let us strive to deserve them better, heartily repenting of all our sins, and especially of our neglect of the means of grace so abundantly vouchsafed to us. In the coming Christmas season, saddened as it will be by the thought of our Queen's sorrows and the national loss, let us give glory to God in the highest for the gift of peace on earth, and good will towards men, in the birth and incarnation of our blessed Lord and Saviour Jesus Christ. Let us labour, as far as in us lies, for peace with all men, abroad and at home. Abroad, if we are forced to draw the sword, let us wield it in the strength of the Lord of Hosts, and gladly sheathe it on the first occasion in the name of the Prince of Peace. At home let us strive charitably, but earnestly, that no man may take from our Queen, our country, and ourselves, that bright crown of a pure Church, preaching Christ in every parish of England, and carrying to heathen lands the same message of salvation. So for us, as for Judah of old, will the Lord 'wait that He may be gracious unto us; so will He be exalted that He may have mercy upon us; for the Lord is a God of judgment: blessed are all they that wait for Him. And though the Lord give us the bread of adversity and the water of affliction, yet shall not our teachers be removed; our eyes shall see our teachers, and our ears shall hear a word behind us, saying, This is the way, walk ye in it, when ye turn to the right hand, and when ye turn to the left.' 'Trust ye in the Lord for ever; for in the Lord Jehovah is everlasting strength.' Amen.

SERMON XVI.

PAPAL SUPREMACY.

OUTLINE OF A SERMON PREACHED IN ST CHAD'S CHURCH, SHREWSBURY, IN THE EVENING OF THURSDAY, APRIL 10, 1851.[1]

EPHES. I. 22-3.

And hath put all things under his feet, and gave him to be Head over all things to the Church, which is his Body.

ST PAUL sets forth the glorified Christ as given to be Head of the Church; the Church as Christ's body. The Church is a communion of saints, visible and invisible, and it has one head, both spiritual and corporeal, divine and human, one Christ, who dwells in glory, but has

---

[1] The Sermon (of which the outline here given appeared in a local Journal) was written as part of a course preached in 1851 by clergymen of Shrewsbury on Roman errors. It occupied two hours and ten minutes in delivery, and was attentively heard by a large congregation.

promised to be with his Church always, wherever two or three are gathered together in his name. Therefore it is blasphemy against Christ to own any other head but this one:—to say that a visible head is required for a visible Church, which is the Roman doctrine.

The supremacy of the Bishop of Rome lies at the foundation of Romanism. If this be overthrown all its unscriptural tenets perish with it. Roman writers, Bellarmine, De Maistre, Perrone, &c., confess as much. The Pope's supremacy was defined at the Council of Florence, 1439, as a "full power to feed, regulate, and govern the Universal Church." In the Canon Law, it is said that no Councils can be summoned without his permission, nor are their resolutions valid until confirmed by him: that the creation and alteration of sees, the translation, deposition, and confirmation of bishops belong only to the Pope: that all greater causes are reserved to him: that the spiritual power is above the temporal: that the Pope can dispense against the Apostles, against positive right: can make unjust things just: can make something out of nothing: that he holds the place of the true God on earth. This presumptuous Canon Law is founded to a great extent on documents now confessed to be frauds and forgeries. The title of Pope, or Father, was originally given to all eminent bishops, and was not confined to the Roman bishops till the 11th century. His other titles, Sovereign Pontiff, Universal Bishop, &c., were usurpations of no early date. There have been two parties in the Roman Church, the moderate and the ultramontane. This latter, which maintains the Pope's infallibility and exaggerates his power to the utmost, is now everywhere dominant, and likely to become so more and more.

Some cautions are necessary in arguing with Romanists: 1. They must not be suffered to quit the ground of Scripture for that of Church authority. 2. They must not be allowed to prejudice the argument by maintaining that a visible head is *necessary* in the Church as a centre of unity. 3. They must not be allowed to confound the terms primacy and supremacy, as they often try to do. We allow a certain primacy (i.e. precedency) to St Peter among apostles, and to Rome among ancient churches: but we deny the supremacy of both. 4. Testimonies must be nicely discriminated.

The Roman doctrine may be reduced to four propositions:—1. That St Peter received a divine right to govern the Church. 2. And to transmit the government to successors. 3. That Peter became Bishop of Rome, and transmitted his right to all future Bishops of Rome. 4. That the Bishops of Rome have always possessed and exercised this right.

1. As to the first proposition, its scriptural evidence must first be examined. Mr Allies (*See of Peter*) puts the Roman case very strongly. It rests mainly on three texts:—Matthew xvi. 13—19; Luke xxii. 31—2; John xxi. 15—17. But the Roman inference from these texts is mere assumption, unsupported by the rest of Scripture and by the Fathers. The texts of Luke and John may be explained from the personal character and history of Peter, and so the Fathers generally explain them. In

the same way that of Matthew is explained. Peter represents the Apostles; confesses for all and receives a blessing first for himself, which is extended however to all. For, if he was to be a rock, or chief agent of Christ in founding the Church, the other Apostles were also to be rocks or foundations, as appears from Ephes. ii. 20; Rev. xxi. 14. Most of the Fathers understood the rock to be Peter's faith, not himself, and the keys, or power of binding and loosing, as given in St Peter to the whole Church, not as a peculiar gift to him. These interpretations are quite as probable as the Roman, and have more authority. But the dogma of Peter's supremacy is invincibly demolished by the following argument: If St Peter had possessed supreme jurisdiction, it must have been known to the inspired and to the primitive writers: if it had been known to them, they would have declared it: but they have not declared it: therefore St Peter did not possess any such jurisdiction. As to the Scriptural writers, they agree in making St Peter first and foremost among the Apostles, but they give him no sovereignty. St Mark, his own disciple, is silent as to any blessing addressed to him. St Luke and St John do not repeat the blessing in Matthew. The Acts exhibit Peter as primate of the Apostles before the conversion of St Paul, but not as sovereign; he is *sent* by the rest, he is called to account by the Jewish Christians and put on his defence: at the Council in Jerusalem St James presides. After St Paul's conversion, Peter almost disappears from the history. If high privileges give supremacy, Paul does not yield to Peter. And in the whole of his writings he gives no hint of Peter's supremacy. Neither do St John, St James, St Jude, or St Peter himself. Again, on examining the Fathers of the first six centuries (whose works might fill 100 folio volumes) we find only two or three passages which would seem to favour this doctrine, and they not only can be otherwise interpreted, but are counteracted by other passages in the same writers evidently hostile to the doctrine. St Peter, therefore, had no supremacy.

2. If he had, there is no proof at all that he had the power of transmitting it.

3. There is no certainty that he ever was Bishop of Rome, or that the Bishops of Rome were his successors. The Roman statement has nothing but vague, suspicious, and inconsistent legends in its favour.

4. The fourth Roman proposition, that the Bishops of Rome have always possessed and exercised supreme power is overthrown by proving the following allegations:—(1) That no such supremacy of the Roman Bishop was recognised by any part of the Church or exercised by him for at least six centuries after Christ; as appears from the writings of the Fathers, the Acts and Canons of Councils, and other records. (2) That the authority subsequently acquired by him in the Western Church appears on the face of it to be a mere human usurpation, achieved by ambitious and politic Popes, seizing favourable opportunities. (3) That the Universal Supremacy of the Roman Bishop never has been really acknowledged and obeyed by the whole Catholic Church; the Greeks having separated from the

Latin Church without any such previous acknowledgment, and having always maintained their independence in spite of concessions wrung from two weak and despairing Emperors in the 13th and 15th centuries. These allegations being proved, the pretensions of Rome fall to the ground.

The claim is also to be rejected for many reasons evincing the unholiness of Papal supremacy: as, the wicked lives of many Popes: the frauds, forgeries, and manifold impostures by which their power has been advanced and maintained: the disparagement of the Holy Scriptures: the introduction of false doctrines and corrupt worship: the cruel, persecuting, and immoral spirit, laws, and dealings of the Papacy: the proceedings of the Dominicans, the Jesuits, and the Inquisition: the revival of the Jesuits after their formal suppression: the evident tendency of Papal influence to bring nations to decay, decrepitude, and ruin. And herein we find a sufficient answer to the modern theory of Development, as advanced by Möhler and Newman. For the growth of Papal power is evidently not the ripening of good seed to good fruit, but the development of an evil germ to maturity of evil, the gradual expansion of a baleful Upas-tree.

The accession of converts to Rome arises chiefly from the specious prejudice, that a visible head is necessary as a centre of unity and judge of controversy in the Church. This is only a plausible sophism: for, (1) it is mere carnal presumption to seize the sceptre from God's hand, and determine for ourselves how He *ought* to have arranged the government of the Church, instead of humbly inquiring what He *has* been pleased to intimate on the subject. May it not with as much probability be supposed that the absence of a central human tribunal of faith is designed to prove the hearts and tempers of men? (2) We may fairly say, in reply to the Romanist, that if God had judged a visible Head so necessary, He would have given to mankind an earlier and more distinct revelation of this doctrine. (3) Roman unity is merely negative and external, for it cannot with truth be said that all members of that Church are really of one heart and one mind, as the first Christians were. (4) Roman unity does not savour of the simplicity and spirituality of the Gospel. Rather it is an artificial organism, like that of Freemasons, Illuminati, or the Fehmic brotherhood, a conspiracy to hold mankind in bondage, not a dispensation of God's free spirit. It is held together by the machinery of Clerical Celibacy, Monastic Institutions, and Auricular Confession; the two former supplying the Pope with a devoted, widespread, and not too scrupulous militia, the last enabling that militia to rule the consciences of the laity, and hold them in vassalage to the Pope. Roman unity, in short, is but the unity of a cleverly organized Priestcraft. (5) And this external unity, such as it is, has not been maintained in the Roman Church. We read of heretic Popes, Popes deposed, Popes and Councils quarrelling, Popes contradicting Popes: varying Papal editions of the Bible: Gallican and Ultramontane factions, Jesuits and Jansenists, Jesuits and Dominicans, in frequent and violent collision: Febronian, Hermesian,

Rongian disputes: and the all important question of infallibility unsettled for more than 18 centuries. What is the practical value of such a unity as this?

If men were not carnal, they might be satisfied with the unity which brought peace to holy men of olden time, to St Basil, for instance, and Cyril of Alexandria. Basil explains unity to consist in the members being joined to each other in one *sole* Head, which is Christ. Cyril, in his discourses on St John (ch. xiv.—xvii.), gives no hint of a mere outward unity, but speaks only of a spiritual union. And yet Cyril was President of the third General Council at Ephesus, in the 5th century after Christ. Let us choose, therefore, the Holy Ghost guiding us, which we will henceforth serve: a carnal unity or a spiritual one: the Pope or Christ: Rome or the Bible—Which?

REASONS FOR ACQUIESCENCE IN THE JUDGMENT DELIVERED BY THE JUDICIAL COMMITTEE OF THE PRIVY COUNCIL, IN THE CASE OF GORHAM v. THE BISHOP OF EXETER.

"For we know in part, and we prophesy in part. But when that which is perfect is come, then that which is in part shall be done away..........And now abideth faith, hope, charity, these three; but the greatest of these is charity."—1 CORINTH. xiii.

"Summa nostrae religionis pax est et unanimitas. Ea vix constare poterit, nisi de quam paucissimis definiamus, et in multis relinquamus suum cuique judicium."—Erasmus. p. 1162, Ed. Bas.

These Reasons were printed in order to explain why I declined to sign a Declaration which received the signatures of a large number of Clergy: and they were introduced by the Preface which follows.

[THE Bishop of Exeter (Philpotts) says, in one of his published Letters to Mr Maskell, that a time is come for individual confessions of faith. This confession of mine, however, is not elicited by his Lordship's suggestion, but by a Declaration hereinafter quoted. Not that I have viewed with careless eye the throes of our Church for many years now past—or ceased to deplore the faults of parties,—or neglected to pray for the peace of our Zion. But, except having occasionally given my silent name to whatever cause, under whatever superscription, appeared to be the cause of Christian liberty, candour, and charity, I have held aloof from controversies in which I had not perfect sympathy with either contending party, and no vocation to be a mediator.

But I find myself now in a new position. I cannot, for the reasons hereinafter stated, unite in this address to our Diocesan. Yet, if I simply withhold my name, I leave it to be supposed either that I belong to an extreme antagonistic School of Divinity, which is not the fact : or that, being a Presbyter of the Church, honoured with a seat in the Cathedral Church of this Diocese, commissioned to teach in theology, and specially to instruct youth, I either have no opinion, or fear to express that opinion, on a question of momentous concern to the Church of Christ: both which suppositions would, again, be untrue.

Thus I feel myself constrained to speak, and I have only to hope that my reasons for doing so will be satisfactory to those whose good opinion I value, whether they agree with me otherwise or not.

The sentiments herein put forth have long been mine; they have grown with my growth and strengthened with my strength; and have been confirmed by all the aids I could employ for the correction of my own judgment. Nevertheless, I commit them to publication with fear and trembling, concerning, as they do, a question of so awful a character, and opposed, as I fear they are, to the feelings of so many good and learned men. And if indeed they be such as justly to offend any of Christ's little ones, I beseech our Divine Head to convince me of my sin, and to give me grace to retract my error.

But, if these opinions originate in truth, and tend to truth, then I pray for grace and strength to maintain and defend them; and I desire to unite in prayer and mutual help with all Churchmen, (some there must be, I trust there are many), whose earnest expectation waits for a Church of the future, in which symbolism[1] shall retire within the narrowest limits consistent with common worship, and the Baptized shall eat the flesh of the Son of Man and drink his blood with unrefining faith, and learn to do his will, that so, by the witness of the Spirit, they may know of his doctrine, that it is indeed from that Father, whose name is Love.]

I, the undersigned, being a Clergyman residing within the Archdeaconry of Salop, in the Diocese of Lichfield, do profess that I cannot in my conscience subscribe the foregoing Declaration for the following reasons:—

1. Because the Judgment of the Judicial Committee of the Privy Council in the case of Gorham *v.* the Bishop of Exeter, appears to import no more than this:—that the said Committee, not sitting as a Tribunal of Faith, but being legally constituted by the Queen's Majesty to try, on appeal, a Question of Ecclesiastical Right involving a Question of Doctrine, applied itself to the careful consi-

---

[1] By the word 'Symbolism' I mean the establishment of Dogmatic Articles as Terms of Communion.

deration of the documentary and historical facts of the case; and having found, as matter of fact, that, from the publication of Articles of Religion to the present day, Divines of the Church of England, Bishops as well as Presbyters, have, without molestation, professed opinions differing from each other in various degrees respecting the effects of Infant Baptism, as also respecting the mode of interpreting the language of the Articles, Liturgy, and Catechism of the Church relating to that question, the said Judicial Committee did simply declare that the doctrine of the Appellant concerning Infant Baptism is not so plainly and certainly opposed to the teaching of the Church, as that he ought, by reason thereof, to be refused Institution to a Cure of Souls.

2. Because it appears that the Judicial Committee could not have pronounced judgment against the Appellant without attainting, by a retrospective sentence, the soundness and honesty of many Divines, who in times past have been regarded as burning and shining lights in the Church of England.

3. Because the principle of charitable presumption, which is used to interpret the language of the Baptismal service by those who deny the unconditional Regeneration of all Infants in and by their Baptism, is not unsanctioned by the example of our Saviour and his Apostles, and does indeed appear to be an essential condition of Common Prayer and Christian fellowship on earth: and, whereas the Thanksgiving in the Service for the Baptism of Persons of Riper Years is avowedly founded on charitable presumption, there would appear to be no

dishonesty in applying the same principle to the Thanksgiving of the other Service, unless it could be shown that the Church has positively declared the Regeneration of Infants in and by their Baptism to be unconditional and absolute.

Because, furthermore, the Church Catechism itself, dogmatic as it is and not liturgical, appears to require the application of the same principle, seeing that all Baptized persons must needs be dealt with by the Church as possessing the privileges of Christian membership, while it is admitted that the Baptism of some Adults is nullified by their want of Repentance and Faith[1].

4. Because it does not appear that from that Article of the Creed called Nicene, which acknowledges one Baptism for the remission of sins, and which St Cyril, in his Catechesis thereupon, scripturally cites as one Baptism of Repentance for the Remission of Sins, we are necessitated to infer the unconditional Remission of Original Sin to all Infants, in and by their Baptism[1].

5. Because our Church, in accordance with Holy Scripture, confines sacramental grace, in general, to such as worthily receive the same; and, whereas the conditions of Baptismal grace, in general, are declared to be Repentance and Faith, which Infants cannot perform, yet it does not seem to follow, as a necessary consequence, that no personal conditions are required in Infants, although none are defined by Scripture and the Church.

6. Because, while it is fully admitted that the Chris-

---

[1] See, however, the concluding Head of this Declaration.

tian Fathers of the first four centuries unanimously represent Baptism as the divinely appointed means of obtaining Remission of Sins and spiritual Regeneration, insomuch that Baptism and Regeneration are with them convertible terms; and although Clement of Alexandria, and, after him, the Fathers of the fourth century, exhaust the riches of their imagination in describing the blessings of the Baptized, yet all these Fathers evidently write with particular regard to Adults, and to such Adults as bring to Baptism the conditions of sincere Repentance and lively Faith.

7. Because, although the practice of baptizing Infants is referred by Origen to apostolical tradition, and is shown by certain testimony to have existed from an early period, yet the Church of the first four centuries appears not to have ranked the Baptism of Infants as of equal importance with that of Adults; seeing that its blessings are nowhere described in the same glowing language; that Tertullian, in the beginning of the third century, while he magnifies highly the gifts of Baptism, does not hesitate to argue against that of Infants; and the Fathers of the fourth century, while they remonstrate earnestly and frequently with Adults against the prevalent custom of delaying their Baptism, do not appear, in general, to have warned Parents of peril incurred by deferring the Baptism of their Infants.

8. Because, if the denial of absolute Infant Regeneration be not exempt from the peril of Zuinglian or of Calvinistic error, its assertion cannot easily be distinguished, even upon the Lutheran hypothesis of Faith

infused in and by Baptism, from the Scholastic theory of grace conferred *ex opere operato;* which theory, if it be once received into any one part of Christian Theology, tends to leaven and determine the whole system.

9. Because the dogma of the unconditional Regeneration of all Infants in and by their Baptism appears to have been shaped during the third and fourth centuries after Christ in one division of the Church Catholic—that of (Western) Africa, and to have become current in the fifth century by means of one extraordinary man, Augustine, whose writings have exercised more important influence in some departments of later Theology, than those of inspired Apostles and Evangelists.

10. Because it is a wise and just ecclesiastical rule, which prescribes Unity in things necessary, Liberty in things doubtful, and Charity in all things ; and because all Churches appear to have erred more or less from this rule by multiplying Articles of Necessity, to the great detriment of Liberty and Charity. And because it seems that a time must arrive for the Church to consider whether Terms of Common Worship which might be necessary in the fifth century, or again in the peculiar circumstances of the English Reformation, will be equally desirable in the third Millennium of the Christian religion ; pending which consideration, the reasonable and just liberties of Churchmen ought to be protected by the State, in whatsoever person or particular they may be endangered.

Nevertheless, although the personal conditions of Infant Salvation appear to me to be among those 'deep things of God,' which, as the Spirit has not revealed them, a Church, not infallible, may leave undefined without deserting its office as a Witness of Truth, and Judge of Controversy ; although, therefore, *a fortiori*, I acquiesce in the modest Judgment pronounced by the Judicial Committee of the Privy Council, I do gladly believe, and would teach all Christian parents to believe, with the Rubric of our Church, that Baptized Infants, dying before they commit actual sin, are undoubtedly saved; and I thankfully accept the authority which our Church gives me in her Catechism to deal practically with Baptized persons as being, in point of privilege and capacity, 'members of Christ, children of God, and inheritors of the Kingdom of Heaven,' and charitably to address even the worldly and wicked among them, not as unregenerate, alien, and uncovenanted persons, but as prodigal sons, unfaithful servants and backsliders, who need repentance, turning to God, and renewing of the Holy Ghost.

SERMON XVII.

THE CHRIST OF PROPHECY.

PREACHED BEFORE THE UNIVERSITY OF CAMBRIDGE,
ON PALM SUNDAY, MARCH 25, 1877.

LUKE XXIV. 25, 26.

Then said he unto them: O fools and slow of heart to believe all that the prophets have spoken! Ought not the Christ to have suffered these things, and to enter into his glory?

WHATEVER grave faults of doctrine, discipline or conduct may be noted in the Christian Church during its progress through eighteen centuries, yet has it preserved to us, under a mercifully guiding Providence, two blessings of priceless worth. In the Bible it has kept for us God's revealed Word to man; that Word which proclaims our moral nature and its meaning; that Word which tells us that we are distinct from the beasts that perish, tells us why and wherein we are so, and how we may continue to be so more and more for ever. And in the services of its Holy Year the Church brings constantly before our view the historical Christ, Him in whom and by whom alone our sin-stained and sin-laden souls have a sure and certain hope of restoration and release, of peace and joy.

The march of the Christian year has brought us to the first day of that which we justly call Holy Week, the Week of our accomplished Redemption. What a vast weight of matter lies within the compass of this Week! What store of meditation for the prayerful Christian student! What wealth of sermons for the faithful Christian preacher!

The miracle of miracles had been wrought under the walls of Jerusalem. The dead had been brought to life: Lazarus had risen from the tomb. All Jewish eyes were now turned with hope or hatred on Jesus of Nazareth: with hope on the expected Deliverer; with hatred on the dreaded Reformer. And this was known to Jesus, and known to his disciples. The Passover was at hand. The twelve intreat their Master to refrain from attending that feast. Their dissuasion is vain. He stedfastly set his face to go from Peræa to Jerusalem. He knew that He was going to die there; and this He foretold to his disciples. Yet did He press on before, while they followed in terror and dismay.

And now, on the Jewish sabbath, He has reached Bethany, the scene of his far-famed miracle. Yet one manifestation of his Messianic character, one hour of kingly glory shall be his, before the day of his deep humiliation. Often with a few friends had He descended the Mount of Olives and entered Jerusalem as the son of the Nazarene carpenter. Now, as on this day, shall

He enter the sinful city and weep over its impending doom, as the Son of David, the expected Christ, escorted, saluted, amidst crowds strewing emblematic palm-branches. He shall enter, but in what guise? Not on caparisoned steed, as a warrior prepared for battle. Not in four-horse chariot, as a conqueror celebrating his triumph. But even such as we see Him in the picture of the prophet Zechariah: 'Rejoice greatly, O daughter of Zion; shout, O daughter of Jerusalem: behold, thy King cometh unto thee; he is just and having salvation; lowly and riding upon an ass, and upon a colt the foal of an ass.'

But not solely for the purpose of fulfilling prophecy do we deem that Jesus thus publicly entered Jerusalem on the day of Palms. Other lessons also He may then have been teaching, more in number perhaps, and some of deeper import, than our poor thought is able to exhaust. Among them we can hardly err if we include the light which the narrative throws upon the vanity of popular applause, and upon the frequent blindness and shallowness of what is boastfully called public opinion. Five days later the same Jesus was led forth before the multitude, a prisoner condemned by the Sanhedrim and in custody of the Roman Procurator. Amidst the vast crowd of Jews, who, replying to Pilate's question, 'Shall I crucify your King?' yelled fiercely, 'Crucify him,' can we doubt that many were present who on the day of Palms had swelled the shout 'Hosanna to the Son of David'? Some indeed might be suborned agents of the Scribes and Pharisees; but more, we suspect, were dupes of their own disappointment, who having sought in Jesus an insurrectionary chief, now repudiated Him as a broken reed, a defeated and useless charlatan.

The events and characters of Holy Week teach lessons for all times and all places: for us and for our times as much as for any other. From the Sanhedrim we learn the wickedness of party spirit; from Pilate the wickedness induced by fear of the world; from the multitude we receive the warning now stated.

The mammon-worshippers in the world around us have a current and vicious proverb: 'Nothing succeeds like success,' which necessarily implies its converse, 'Nothing fails like failure.' To the Jewish malcontents who thronged Pilate's prætorium on the Friday, Jesus of Nazareth seemed indeed to have failed utterly; to be crushed by the shame and ruin of the impending cross. Therefore they yelled fiercely against Him; therefore, when asked by Pilate, 'Whom shall I release unto you?' they spat their venom against Jesus, crying, 'Not this man, but Barabbas.'

Brethren, ere we pass on, let us ask ourselves, whether from the Cross of that Redeemer, whose name we bear, we have learnt the contrary lesson, even the dignity, the grandeur, the victory, the triumph of godly suffering? Do we, from principle and habit, take up our cross, and follow Him whithersoever He points the way, to whatsoever earthly fate?

But leaving for other preachers the throng of events in this week, until on Holy Thursday the Christian

Church was first founded by the institution of the perpetual Communion of the Founder's Body and Blood (a foundation completed after his resurrection by the mission of his apostles to teach and baptize in every nation) —leaving the scenes of that awful drama which ensued, from the Agony in the garden and the Redemption finished on Calvary, even to the hour when the mysterious darkness of the Saviour's tomb was scattered by the glorious sun of Easter, and Death and Hell resigned their mightier prey—we pass on to the scene from which my text is taken. That scene occurs on the afternoon of Easter Sunday: and the words were spoken by our Lord after his resurrection to the two disciples whom He joined as they were walking to Emmaus.

These disciples had seen the wonderful miracles which Jesus wrought during his lifetime, and, like Nicodemus, they knew that he was a Teacher come from God; seeing that no man could do the miracles which He did except God were with him. This knowledge and persuasion doubtless they still retained. But their hopes and their belief respecting the person of Jesus had gone much farther than this. To use their own words, they trusted it had been He which should have redeemed Israel; they had thought that Jesus was the Christ or Messiah, the great subject of prophecy, the promised Seed of the woman, the desire of all nations. This trust had now failed them, and the reason was, that they had not rightly understood the prophecies and types of Messiah. They had not been prepared by these, as they might have been, to expect that the

Christ would undergo the sufferings which they had recently witnessed in the case of Jesus of Nazareth. Nor even after the event did they recognize, as they ought to have done, the fulfilment of what the Prophets had spoken. Accordingly, while they still knew, from his miracles, that Jesus had been a teacher come from God, they had ceased to regard Him as the Christ of prophecy. This drew from our blessed Lord, who was as yet unknown to them, the reproving words of the text, 'O fools and slow of heart to believe all that the prophets have spoken! ought not the Christ to have suffered these things, and to enter into his glory?'

A slight paraphrase may avail to place in clearer and stronger light these momentous words of our Lord, to which our current version hardly does justice. He says: 'O ye whose understandings are not yet opened, whose hearts are not yet quickened enough, to have faith in all the sayings which the prophets spake: was it not necessary to the fulfilment of those sayings that the Messiah should suffer these things, which Jesus of Nazareth has now suffered, and then, not till then, should enter into his glory?'

After this appeal (the Evangelist goes on to say), 'beginning at Moses and all the prophets' (that is, from the writings of all the prophets from Moses downwards) He expounded unto them in all the scriptures the things concerning Himself.'

The things which our Lord taught to his disciples He would have his ministers preach to their congregations in all time to come. And although from a pulpit like this his minister is addressing many whose understandings have been opened to know, and whose hearts are quick to feel, the things concerning Him, yet it is good for the wisest and the best to review their knowledge from time to time, and to revive their Christian feelings continually.

Let us then now with humble and uplifted thoughts pray that our divine Redeemer will be pleased to open our understandings wider still, and quicken our hearts yet more vividly by his Holy Spirit, while we strive to recall some of the testimonies which God has given to us in all his Scriptures by the inspired voices of his prophets, by the ordinances of his law, and by typical prefigurations, that the Christ was to suffer and die; and that the very kind of his sufferings, and the very manner of his death, were not unannounced, but, as they were certainly foreknown by Him who knoweth the end from the beginning, so were they also foretold in the writings of the first covenant.

I. The prophecies which represent Messiah under the general character of a sufferer are too numerous for citation, and most of them too well known to render citation necessary.

How it was declared seven hundred years before Jesus was born, that Messias should be 'a man of sorrows and acquainted with grief,' that He should be 'stricken, smitten of God and afflicted,' all will recollect. And to add one typical person as predictive of the same sufferings, thus verbally foretold, you know how many are the afflictions of which David complains, in words far more closely applicable to the lot of Christ than to his own ; how he speaks of himself as 'grieved because of the transgressors, because they kept not God's law ;' how as the type of Christ he said, 'The zeal of thine house hath eaten me up;' and again, 'My God, my God, why hast thou forsaken me?'

But further, that the sufferings of the Christ were not to fall short of death, is a fact everywhere recognised in the Old Testament, more especially in the whole series of Levitical sacrifices, which in various ways prefigured the offices of Christ and the benefits which we receive thereby : everywhere with this one circumstance strongly marked, that those his offices were to be fulfilled at the expense of his life, and that these our benefits were to be purchased by his blood.

But in order that the purpose and end of prophecy might be answered, God did not declare, in such terms as might be clearly understood before the event, how Messiah should be cut off. And we can hardly doubt that the Priests would have allowed Jesus to live, or would have contrived for Him another manner of death, rather than have afforded such full evidence of the truth of his claim, by the very indignities with which they loaded Him and in the accursed death which they prepared for Him.

It was necessary therefore that the prophecies respecting Christ's death should be equally obscure before, and plain after, the event; that they should be such as could be explained afterwards of no other manner of execution, and of no other person who suffered the same sentence,

except the Christ, yet that beforehand they should be
so announced as not to shew themselves evidently descriptive of such a manner of execution. And in accordance with these requirements, while nothing can be more
remote in the form of description, nothing can more
truly describe or more fully distinguish the manner of
Christ's death—both in its great features and in its minor
incidents, both where it resembled and where it differed
from the death of others condemned to the same sufferings—than those types and predictions which we now refer
with full assurance to the Crucifixion of Jesus the Son of
the Virgin Mary.

II. If it was prophesied by Isaiah that the Christ
should 'be taken from prison and from judgment,' we
know that Jesus was apprehended like a thief and suffered by a judicial sentence.

If it was said by a type of Messiah 'False witnesses
did rise up, they laid to my charge things that I knew
not'—so also 'many bare false witness against Jesus, but
their witness agreed not together.'

If it was foretold of the Christ, that 'as a sheep before
her shearers is dumb, so he opened not his mouth,'—we
know that 'when Jesus was accused of the Chief Priests
and Elders he answered nothing,' and again before Pilate
'he answered him to never a word, insomuch that the
Governor marvelled greatly.'

Had it been declared that Messiah was 'just' and
'had done no violence'? His very judge said of Jesus,
'What evil hath he done?' 'I find no fault in him.'

Moreover, to one only kind of death, out of all those

that had been judicially inflicted in any nation, could the predictive allusions of Christ's death refer; they all point to crucifixion, and by crucifixion Jesus suffered.

Scourging was a part of the punishment which those underwent who were condemned to the cross; and accordingly it had been said in the prophets, 'with his stripes we are healed,' 'I gave my back to the smiters,' and again, 'the ploughers ploughed upon my back and made long furrows;' and we read that 'Pilate took Jesus and scourged him.'

It was customary that he, who was to be suspended on the tree, himself carried the instrument of his execution; and Isaac, that well-known type of Christ, 'bare the wood for his sacrifice,' thus pointing to crucifixion. And Jesus, though He did not bear it all the way, yet, as St John writeth, 'went forth bearing his cross.'

If the cruelty of this method of execution moved compassion so general that a cup of bitter anodyne was usually presented to the sufferer, we find David alluding to crucifixion, when he says, 'They gave me gall for my meat, and when I was thirsty they gave me vinegar to drink.' And so in the fulfilment by Jesus, 'they gave him vinegar to drink mingled with gall.'

If the hands and feet of a crucified person were pierced, the Psalmist had already said 'They pierced my hands and my feet.' And Thomas actually thrust his fingers into the prints of the nails on the body of Jesus.

And once more, as the body thus fastened upon the tree was lifted up and presented to the gaze of men, so was the brazen serpent in the wilderness. "Moses put it upon a pole, and it came to pass that if a serpent had bitten any man, when he beheld the serpent of brass he lived.' And in full accordance with this was Jesus lifted up, to save and cure us from the deadly poison infused into us by the bite of the Old Serpent, as He prophesied of Himself: 'As Moses lifted up the serpent in the wilderness, even so must the Son of Man be lifted up, that whosoever believeth in Him should not perish, but have eternal life.'

III. Thus surely did the ancient types and prophecies point to the crucifixion of Messiah, by mentioning or alluding to the circumstances which usually accompany that punishment; and as surely were they all made yea and amen in the person of Jesus of Nazareth.

And yet that the Messiah, He whom David called Lord, should be crucified, and that too in pursuance of a judicial sentence—how opposite to all preconceived expectations! For when we look upon Messiah as the Son of God, and remember the malediction, 'Cursed is every one that hangeth on a tree,' there seems something in the sanctity of that person and office incompatible with such a death, the death of a criminal slave.

And again, that Jesus was thus crucified, and that as a convict of justice, how passing strange! For, when we remember the innocency of Jesus, and the offence laid to his charge, to which stoning, not crucifixion, was the punishment awarded by his own nation, and by the very law which his accusers cited against Him, when they said, 'We have a law, and by that law he ought to die;' when we bear these things in mind, it seems alike improbable, that Jesus, the innocent and holy, should suffer as a criminal, and that sentenced as a blasphemer He should be crucified as a malefactor. To make this possible, a long course of events had preceded, not indeed in their own nature what we call miraculous, but which we may certainly affirm that Omniscience alone could have foreseen. The sceptre had departed from Judah, and the power of life and death had been taken from the Jewish tribunals; and therefore, as the Jews dared not put in execution their own sentence against Him for blasphemy, they were obliged to denounce Jesus to the Roman Procurator as a rebel; and thus was the Christ, born a Jew after the flesh, condemned by a Roman law and executed with a Roman death. How unsearchable are the judgments of God, and his ways past finding out! Yet, had not the understandings of the Jews been blinded by the malice of their hearts, their own actions and their own words might have taught them that Jesus was indeed the Christ. They found themselves forced to have recourse to foreign legislation; and they cried out, 'We have no king but Cæsar;' thus bearing witness, by their own deeds and with their own tongues, to the presence of Messiah. For had not their own Moses left them this prophetic record, 'The sceptre shall not depart from Judah, nor a lawgiver from between his feet, till Shiloh come'?

But thus it ever is, O Lord, that even the wrath of man is made to praise Thee!

'The kings of the earth stood up, and the rulers were gathered together against the Lord, and against his Christ; for of a truth against thy holy child Jesus, whom Thou hast anointed, both Herod and Pontius Pilate, with the Gentiles and the people of Israel, were gathered together, for to do whatsoever thy hand and thy counsel determined before to be done.'

IV. If time allowed, I might go on to shew that even those which might be deemed the accidental circumstances of the death of Jesus were not so left to the malice or carelessness of his executioners, as no longer to be found strangely obedient to a voice of past ages. Whether his enemies act before a public tribunal, or in a secret cabal, whether they use the solemnity of an appointed judge, or the unseemly violence of a mob, equally do they fulfil all that the prophets have spoken, equally do they give effect to the revealed counsel of Jehovah. Where they hold their hand, and where they strike, equally are they obedient in rebellion, equally servants in their licentious freedom. Whether they observe or whether they forego a custom; whether they neglect or whether they insult their victim; in all that the Prophets have spoken we find that the Christ ought to have suffered—was to suffer—these very things.

Call to mind these particulars, my brethren: the wicked bargain of the traitor Judas; the thirty pieces of silver; the shame and spitting; the suffering without the gate; the time of death, even that when the Paschal Lamb was slain; the crucifixion between two thieves; their taunts and the taunts of the crowd; the withdrawal of disciples and friends; the casting of lots for the raiment of Jesus; the piercing of his side, while his legs remained unbroken: —all these things (you will remember) were foretold in the prophetic writings of the Old Testament. Well might our blessed Lord reprove the two disciples and say: 'O ye whose minds and hearts are not yet quickened to believe all that the Prophets have spoken, ought not the Christ to have suffered these things?'

V. Such a review of the fulfilment of prophecy in the sufferings and death of our Lord Jesus Christ is calculated to impress many great truths on our minds and hearts. But there are two deductions especially which the writers of the New Testament delight to draw from it: and with these let us now content ourselves.

They repeatedly deduce evidences of our holy religion, and also proofs of the sovereign Providence of God and the subservience of all human devices to his good will and pleasure.

They deduce evidences of Christianity. And even such a concise view of this wide subject as we have now taken should suffice to constrain us who see the fulfilled prophecies, to exclaim, like the people who saw the miracles which Jesus did: 'This is of a truth that Prophet that should come into the world.' But while we imitate them in making this good confession, let us see to it that we do not imitate their instability. We must hold fast the profession of our faith without wavering, being grounded and settled in the truth. And in order to this we must search the Scriptures, to see whether these things be so, and to be able to give a reason to ourselves and others of the hope that is in us. And above all we must remember that more is necessary than mere intellectual research; though that also is required of us in due proportion and according to our measure. For in matters of religion the heart is even more concerned than the understanding. moral aptitude is even more essential than intellectual perception. It is with the heart that man believeth unto righteousness, and spiritual things must be spiritually discerned. Accordingly it is only the pure in heart to whom God reveals—we might almost say can reveal—Himself. The secret of the Lord is with them that fear Him, and He will shew them his covenant. It is he that doeth the will, to whom it is promised that he shall know of the doctrine, whether it be of God.

And lastly, we may learn from this subject how important it is that we should submit ourselves wholly to God's most holy will and pleasure, both actively and passively. God not only works ever by means, but turns every thing and every person to account in the course of his Providence. But then, though all are alike subservient, so far as his purpose and glory are concerned, how unlike their subservience in respect of their own will and their own happiness! How different in their subordination to the divine plan for the salvation of a lost world, were the traitor Judas, the cowardly Pilate, the malicious Priests, the violent and inconstant Jews, on the one hand—and on the other the little band of disciples, going about through evil report and through good, unfurling everywhere the banner of the Cross.

The wonderful arrangement and stability of Jehovah's purposes, with the perfect subordination of every thing, rational and irrational, good and bad, designedly and undesignedly obedient, are thus exemplified most marvellously in the death of Jesus. But they are not less really, though less visibly true, in every passing event. What a noble foundation is this for implicit reliance on the governing and protecting care of the Almighty! Men of all kinds, good and bad, are busily engaged upon the surface of the tide of affairs, moving about like barks that skim the bosom of the deep: but the Providence of God is below, like those mighty undercurrents of the ocean which perform his behests in the physical world with an energy, noiseless indeed and to us obscure, but constant as the course of ages, and more stable than the solid bars of the earth through which they sweep. All we have to do is, to love God, and surrender ourselves unreservedly to his will, and then all things shall work together for our good, and shall ultimately perform even our own pleasure.

If our heart be right with God; if we continue in the faith, and constantly endeavour, in matters of practice as well as of belief, to learn the will of God, and to do it; then have we as sure a confidence that no machinations of men or of spirits can prevail against us, as we have that God's purpose shall stand in any the most important matter. We know that heaven and earth, and the powers of darkness themselves, shall finally achieve that, and that alone, which is agreeable to the counsels and designs of an all-powerful, all-gracious, and all-wise God.

APPENDIX I.

PSALMS AND HYMNS

TRANSLATED AND ORIGINAL.

PSALMS AND HYMNS.

God be merciful unto us. Ps. lxvii.

O GRANT us, God of love,
the blessings of thy grace;
reveal to us from heaven above
the brightness of thy face;
so shall thy way on earth be known,
thy mercy to the nations shown.

Thee let the people praise;
all people unto Thee
sing praise, o God; the kingdoms raise
a shout of holy glee:
for Thou shalt judge mankind aright,
a ruling and a guiding Light.

Thee for thy bounteous hand
let all the people bless,
o God, who givest to the land
its teeming fruitfulness.
still may thy favour on us rest,
and earth in fearing God be blest.

Love is the fulfilling of the Law. Rom. xiii.

WORSHIP God, and Him alone,
to his Name be reverence shown:
pious hearts will soar above;
piety is born of Love,
piety without a flaw;
Love it is fulfils the Law.

unto parents honour show,
and be good to all below:
kindly hearts are dear above;
kindliness is born of Love,
kindliness without a flaw:
Love it is fulfils the Law.

keep thy hands from bloodshed free,
let thy tongue from slander flee:
gentle hearts repose above;
gentleness is born of Love,
gentleness without a flaw:
Love it is fulfils the Law.

covet not thy neighbour's wife,
dearest treasure of his life:
pure hearts see their God above;
purity is born of Love,
purity without a flaw:
Love it is fulfils the Law.

covet not thy neighbour's wealth;
meek content is joy and health:
lowly hearts shall reign above;
lowliness is born of Love,
lowliness without a flaw:
Love it is fulfils the Law.

God is Love: and He hath given
Faith and Hope as guides to heaven:
Faith and Hope shall cease above;
life itself will then be Love,
endless life without a flaw,
Love the one eternal Law.

That ye may abound in hope. Rom. xv.

HOPE, Christian soul; in every stage
of this thine earthly pilgrimage
let heavenly joy thy thoughts engage:
                abound in hope.

hope, though thy lot be want and woe,
though hate's rude storms against thee blow;
thy Saviour's lot was such below:
                abound in hope.

hope, for to them that meekly bear
his cross, he gives his crown to wear;
abasement here is glory there:
                abound in hope.

hope; though thy dear ones round thee die,
behold, with faith's illumined eye,
their blissful home beyond the sky:
                abound in hope.

hope; for upon that happy shore
sorrow and sighing will be o'er,
and saints shall meet to part no more:
                abound in hope.

hope through the watches of the night;
hope till the morrow bring thee light;
hope till thy faith be lost in sight:
                abound in hope.

Behold, I come quickly. Rev. xxii.

SAVIOUR of the nations, come;
leave for us thy glorious home:
glad hosannas we will sing,
greeting Thee, our heavenly King.

come, Lord Jesu, take thy rest
in the convert sinner's breast;
make the quickened heart thy throne,
Son of God, the Virgin's Son.

welcome to this vale of tears,
ripeness of the perfect years,
born as man with men to dwell,
come, our true Immanuel.

God in man, incarnate God,
sinless Child of flesh and blood,
man in God, thy brethren we,
raise us up to God in Thee.

Behold, thy King cometh unto thee. Zech. ix.

ZION, at thy shining gates,
lo, the King of Glory waits:
haste thy Monarch's pomp to greet,
strew thy palms before his feet.

Christ, for Thee their triple light
faith and hope and love unite:
this the beacon we display
to proclaim thine Advent-day.

come, and give us peace within;
loose us from the bands of sin;
give us grace thy yoke to wear,
give us strength thy cross to bear.

make us thine in deed and word,
thine in heart and life, o Lord;
plant in us thy lowly mind,
keep us faithful, loving, kind.

so, when Thou shalt come again,
judge of angels and of men,
we with all thy saints shall sing
hallelujahs to our King.

Abide with us, for it is toward evening. Luke xxiv

AH Jesu Christ, with us abide,
for now, behold, 'tis eventide:
and bring, to cheer us through the night,
thy Word, our true and only light.

in times of trial and distress
preserve our truth and stedfastness,
and pure unto the end, o Lord,
vouchsafe thy Sacraments and Word.

o Jesu Christ, thy Church sustain;
our hearts are wavering, cold, and vain:
then let thy Word be strong and clear
to silence doubt and banish fear.

the days are evil: all around
strife, errors, blasphemies abound,
and secret slander's withering eye,
and soft-tongued, sleek hypocrisy.

from these and all of God abhorr'd,
o Christ, protect us by thy Word;
increase our faith and hope and love,
and bring us to thy fold above.

Watch ye therefore. Matt. xxv..

WHILE the careless world is sleeping,
blest the servants who are keeping
   watch, according to his Word,
   for the coming of their Lord.

at his table He will place them,
with his royal banquet grace them,
   banquet that shall never cloy,
   bread of life and wine of joy.

heard ye not your Master's warning?
He will come before the morning,
   unexpected, undescried;
   watch ye for Him open-eyed.

teach us so to watch, Lord Jesus;
from the sleep of sin release us;
   swift to hear Thee let us be,
   meet to enter in with Thee.

In Him was Life, and the Life was the Light of men.
            1 John i.

O JESU, Light of heavenly day,
the shades of darkness chase away;
lead back the feet, that wildered roam,
to thy true fold, their happy home.

o let the deaf thy trumpet hear,
the dumb proclaim thy coming near;
to icy breasts thy warmth impart,
and melt the sinner's flinty heart.

o Lord, give sight unto the blind;
inform the rude and thoughtless mind;
the scattered tribes recall to Thee;
the wavering souls from doubt set free.

to all the hope of glory seal,
that all, as one, thy truths may feel,
all keep one heaven-directed road,
one faith, one Saviour, and one God.

so they who sing thy praise above
shall knit with us the bands of love,
and Thee for all thy grace adore
in heaven and earth for evermore.

Give the King thy Judgments, o God. Ps. lxxii.

O GOD, whose gifts alone can bless,
thy judgments let the King possess;
give the King's Son thy righteousness.

his word shall judge thy people well,
his doom the sorrows shall dispel
of such as mourn in Israel.

rest for the people shall be shed
from every mountain's shining head,
and o'er the hills by truth be spread.

for He shall end the poor man's woes,
win for the sons of want repose,
and crush the malice of their foes.

He shall come down upon the plain,
as on the mown grass drops the rain,
as showers that water herb and grain.

the just shall flourish in his day,
and peace shall rule with ample sway,
even till the moon shall fade away.

before his everlasting throne
praise God the Father, God the Son,
and God the Spirit, Three in One.

Of such is the kingdom of God. Mark x.

O HIGHEST Love, in lowliest guise
   to this our fallen world displayed,
may I discern with cleansèd eyes
   the Godhead in our flesh arrayed!

o Love, the very Word of God,
   content an infant shape to wear,
and in a stable's mean abode
   to shield Thee from the wintry air;

o Babe divine, before thy face
   be mine to bow the thankful knee,
and by thy soul-converting grace
   become myself a child in Thee!

no more a servant, may I feel
   my heart thy Spirit's blest abode,
and crying 'Abba, Father,' kneel
   a son through Thee, an heir of God.

I bring you tidings of great joy, which shall be to all people. Luke ii.

ALL my heart with joy is springing,
   while in air everywhere
angel choirs are singing.
hark, I hear their joyful ditty:
   'Christ,' they say, 'came to-day,
born in David's city.'

to this lower world descendeth
   from above He whose love
all our sorrows endeth:
He, who breath and being gave us,
   quits the skies, lives and dies
in our flesh to save us:

Christ, our Lamb so meek and loving,
   dries our tears, calms our fears,
all our sins removing:
Christ our Lamb, who suffers for us,
   He can quell death and hell,
and to peace restore us.

hope He brings and consolation,
   from all woes sweet repose,
strength against temptation:
for the ills that men inherit
   Christ can feel, Christ will heal
every wounded spirit.

dear Redeemer, knit Thee to us;
   quelling sin, reign within;
with thy grace renew us:
let us here, on Thee depending,
   in Thee die, with Thee fly
to the bliss unending.

And she brought forth her first-born Son, and wrapped Him in swaddling-clothes, and laid Him in a manger.' Luke ii.

O MIRACLE of mighty love!
the Lord of countless hosts above
  a naked infant lieth:
    for us his birth,
    for us on earth
  He dwelleth, suffereth, dieth.

o Christ, thy glorious poverty
makes all thy people rich in Thee:
  to wealth untold it leads them:
    with heavenly wine
    and bread divine
  thy thirst and hunger feeds them.

ye saints on earth, no more be sad:
this holy Babe will make you glad
  with joy that knows no measure:
    his life above
    is peace and love,
  and pure unfading pleasure.

then let your hearts be bold and strong
to echo forth the angel song:—
  'glory to God be given;
    on earth be peace,
    nor ever cease
  goodwill to men from heaven.'

The government shall be upon his shoulder. Isai. ix.

> To us this day is born a Child
> of a Virgin mother mild:
> to us this day a Son is given,
> our Redeemer sent from heaven.
>
> the government of all things made
> on his shoulder shall be laid:
> He shall be called the Wonderful,
> Lord of boundless endless rule.
>
> the name of Counsellor He bears,
> who the Father's counsel shares.
> He is the mighty God indeed,
> strong to help in all our need.
>
> an everlasting Father, He
> loves us truly, tenderly;
> the Prince of peace, by whom is given
> peace of mind and peace with heaven.
>
> then praise we, with the heav'nly host,
> Father, Son and Holy Ghost,
> abiding through eternity,
> Three in One and One in Three.

As for thy years, they endure throughout all generations.
Ps. cii.

> By Thee, o God, arose the earth,
>   its deep foundations Thou hast laid;
> from Thee the heavens derived their birth,
>   thy skill their mighty fabric made.

they wane, they perish; Thou at rest
    abidest ever underanged;
they fade like raiment; as a vest
    Thou changest them, and they are changed;

but Thou, the unchanging, Thou art He
    whose years run on their endless race:
thy faithful seed shall dwell with Thee,
    thy saints shall stand before thy face.

Thee God supreme, the Father, Son
    and Holy Spirit, we revere;
the One in Three, the Three in One,
    Creator, Saviour, Comforter.

As for man, his days are as grass. Ps. ciii.

THE life of man is like the grass;
his blooming days, as field-flowers, pass:
the north wind blows; their pride is o'er;
the place that knew them knows no more.
but still the Lord from age to age
sustains his holy heritage:
his happy saints behold his grace,
his truth their children's latest race,
who keep his righteous judgments still,
and live obedient to his will.

the Lord in heaven hath set his throne;
He rules o'er all, supreme, alone.
o ye his angels, praise the Lord,
ye warriors strong, who do his word:
all ye who listen to his voice,
and in his glorious works rejoice.

praise ye the Lord, his hosts of light,
who serve Him in the heavenly height:
praise ye the Lord, where'er ye roll,
bright wanderers. praise the Lord, my soul.

Lord, make me to know mine end. Ps. xxxix.

LORD, let me know mine end,
   teach me the measure of my days:
the life on earth I spend,
   how soon its little light decays.
a cypher are my times with Thee,
for man is nought but vanity.

man is a shade, no more;
   he is disquieted in vain;
he heaps his wealthy store,
   nor knoweth whose shall be the gain.
what trust I then?—thy gracious Word.
release me from my sins, o Lord.

lest fools deride, I stand
   silent and calm beneath thy blow:
yet hold thy smiting hand:
   for, when Thou chastenest sin with woe,
our joyless life is worn away,
and men, as by the moth, decay.

Lord, hearken to my prayer,
   give ear unto my weeping cry;
even as my fathers were,
   a pilgrim in the world am I.
then frown no more, but cheer and bless
my parting from this wilderness.

The smoke ascendeth for ever and ever. Rev. xiv.

Ah, dying sinner, think on death,
that last dark hour of failing breath;
repent, amend, and ready be
to face the great eternity.

though all the world were now thine own,
its amplest wealth, its brightest crown,
crown, wealth, and life must quickly flee:
what then remains? eternity.

hark, the last trumpet smites thine ear:
'awake, arise: the Judge is near:'
o tremble, sinner; for to thee
his doom will stamp eternity.

be timely wise: in Christ's true faith
abide, and shun the second death;
so shall thy soul from guilt be free,
and live throughout eternity.

what eye can tell the starry train,
the drops that fill the watery main?
yet these have tale, the stars, the sea:
thy years have none, eternity.

bethink thee, sinner, o'er and o'er,
how dread a word is 'evermore':
time hath an end; but who shall see
the ending of eternity?

Arise, shine, for thy light is come. Isai. lx.

Awake; new light upon thee dawns;
  delay, my soul, no more:
the star of morning bids thee rise
  and ope the lingering door.

it calls thee to another land,
  to joys untold, unpriced;
it leads thee to a Babe divine,
  thy Saviour, Jesus Christ.

He is the branch of Jesse's stem,
  the rose of Sharon's mead;
He is the very Lamb of God,
  and David's royal seed.

when thou hast found that holy Babe,
  in faith before Him fall;
to Him thy treasures yield, to Him
  thy love, thy life, thy all.

for He will speed thee on, fulfill'd
  with his refreshing grace,
to find a better fatherland,
  a happier dwelling-place.

He points to seats beyond the skies,
  the mansions of the blest,
where tyrants persecute no more,
  and holy pilgrims rest.

*They presented unto Him gifts, gold, and frankincense,
and myrrh.* Matt. ii.

O BLESSED Babe divine,
   what offerings shall we give Thee?
the gold of faith be thine :
   for we will still believe Thee.
o fill our eager hearts
   with thy refreshing grace,
and make them fit to be
   thy chosen dwelling-place.

let frankincense be there,
   pure sighs of contrite sadness,
that rise to God in prayer
   for pardon, peace, and gladness.
o make them purer yet,
   and send thy Spirit down
the altar of our hearts
   with holy fire to crown.

and myrrh too we prepare,
   our bitter tribulation,
such grief as Thou didst bear
   for us and our salvation.
be strength and courage ours
   in toil and tears and pain
with Thee to wear the yoke,
   the cross with Thee sustain.

lo, all of ours is thine,
   each hope and thought and feeling :
come, blessèd Babe divine,
   Thyself in us revealing.

to Thee, and God in Thee,
  our dearest wishes tend:
o make us thine and his
  through ages without end.

*We are more than conquerors through Christ that
    strengtheneth us.* Rom. viii.

LABOUR ever, late and early,
  thou that strivest for the crown:
hard the Christian battle, dearly
  wins the warrior his renown.
none but he, the faithful-hearted,
victor from the field hath parted;
    none but he whose love is strong
    sings at last the triumph-song.

thus, o Christ, thy martyrs holy
  fought the fight in ancient time:
dire and dark and melancholy
  went those years of blood and crime:
from the rage of pagan error,
from the trial and the terror
    Thou hast freed us: and no more
    reeks the soil with Christian gore.

Thou hast conquered, Lord of glory:
  evil powers were foiled by Thee;
Calvary, with its awful story,
  tells thy crowning victory.
death by dying was defeated,
life in losing life completed,
    when the Sufferer bowed his head,
    saying, 'It is finishèd.'

o mysterious scene! o wonder
high above our mortal ken!
lost in love and awe we ponder
  Him—the Man who died for men,
Him who drained the cup of anguish
not in rocky tomb to languish,
    but on angel wings to rise
    to his triumph in the skies.

what are human toil and sadness
  to that hour of deadly strife?
what to that eternal gladness
  fleeting joys of earthly life?
live with Him, thyself denying,
die with Him, the cross defying,
    rise with Him, and throned on high
    swell the song of victory.

Who shall separate us from the love of Christ?
  Rom. viii.

A FAITHFUL friend awaits in heaven
  his people friendless and forlorn,
who with a sinful world have striven,
  and bear, like Him, its cruel scorn.
on Jesus all their hopes depend;
for Jesus is a faithful friend.

like to a reed the world is shaken,
  our rock abides for ever fast:
forgotten here, opprest, mistaken,
  we find Him stedfast to the last.
to Jesus all our longings tend,
for Jesus is a faithful friend.

like to a vane, the world still follows
    the shifting gales of wealth and power;
and worldly friends, as summer swallows,
    forsake us in our darkest hour.
but Jesus loves us to the end,
for Jesus is a faithful friend.

for us He bore reproach and anguish,
    for us He died upon the tree:
He left us not in bonds to languish,
    but paid our debt and set us free.
in Jesus truth and mercy blend,
for Jesus is a faithful friend.

then keep thy pomp and idle pleasure,
    thy friends, a light and fickle brood:
in thee, false world, is not our treasure;
    we change thee for a nobler good:
to God in Jesus we ascend,
our faithful, our eternal friend.

They ceased, and there was a calm.   Luke viii.

IN sorrow's darkest, dreadest hour,
when conscience speaks with thrilling power,
when earthly counsel profits nought,
and human aid is vainly sought,
what comfort else can life afford,
but, with the saints who love the Lord,
to fall before our Saviour's face,
and humbly seek his pardoning grace;

to lift the tearful, trembling eye
to God's great mercy-seat on high,
in hope that whispered words of peace
may come and bid our terrors cease:

that He, by whose o'ermastering will
waves sank to sleep, and winds were still,
may soothe the conflict of the breast,
and lull tempestuous woes to rest?

o Lord, amid the roaring sea
our only trust we place in Thee:
from out the depths to Thee we call;
our fears are great, our strength is small.
thy constant love, thy tender care,
alone can save us from despair:
o let us hear through storm and shade
thy voice: "'Tis I; be not afraid.'

I will put a new spirit within you. Ezek. xi.

SIN-LADEN, weary, lost, I flee,
Saviour of sinners, unto Thee,
whose death upon the dismal tree
   won life for dying men:
guilt half-repented and abhorr'd,
self half-subdued I bring, o Lord,
a half-roused heart:—speak Thou the word,
   and I shall live again.

o, by thy warning Spirit show
the pains and terrors here below,
and all the pangs of future woe,
   that wait the unforgiven;
so shall I kneel, and weep, and pray,
and use salvation's fleeting day
to find by Thee, the living Way,
   forgiveness, peace, and heaven.

There is no other God that can deliver after this sort.
Dan. iii.

WHO trusts in God a strong abode
  in heaven and earth possesses;
who looks in love to Christ above,
  no fear his heart oppresses.
in only Thee, dear Lord, we see
  sweet hope and consolation,
our shield from foes, our balm for woes,
  our great and sure salvation.

though Satan's wrath beset our path,
  and worldly scorn assail us,
while Thou art near we shall not fear,
  our faith will never fail us.
thy rod and staff shall keep us safe
  and guide our steps for ever;
nor shade of death nor hell beneath
  our souls from Thee shall sever.

in all the strife of mortal life
  our feet shall stand securely;
temptation's hour shall lose its power,
  for Thou wilt guard us surely.
o God, renew with heavenly dew
  our body, soul and spirit,
until we stand at thy right hand
  by Jesu's saving merit.

So run that ye may obtain. 1 Cor. ix.

ONWARD, holy champion,
  run the Christian race;
leave the world behind thee,
  heavenward set thy face;

fresh from cleansing water,
bright with grace divine,
trained with wholesome nurture,
heavenly bread and wine.

onward, holy champion,
throw all weight aside,
all distracting pleasure,
all encumbering pride :
shun the subtle pitfalls
of the tempter's spite;
let not smiles allure thee,
let not frowns affright.

onward, holy champion ;
angels gazing down
watch thy brave endeavour,
guard thy future crown.
Christ, thy gracious Saviour,
cheers thy striving soul,
and thy prize awaits thee
at the heavenly goal.

My soul is exceeding sorrowful unto death.
Mark xiv.

IN all temptation let us turn,
dear Saviour, unto Thee,
and by the light of faith discern
thy sad Gethsemane.

the big cold drops upon thy brow,
thine agony, thy prayer,
o keep them in our hearts, that Thou
may'st reign for ever there.

the sweet remembrance of that love
   in every trying hour
send, like an angel from above,
   to quell the tempter's power.

so, Saviour, shall our hearts be true
   in life and death to Thee,
enabled by thy grace to view
   thy sad Gethsemane.

It is finished. Joh. xix.

'Tis finishèd: o glorious word
last uttered by the dying Lord!
remember to thy final hour,
my ransomed soul, that word of power:
the Man who died to save thee said
upon his Cross, ''tis finishèd.'

'tis finishèd: upon that Tree
the Law, the Prophecies we see
in Jesu's bleeding form fulfilled,
e'en as of old Jehovah willed:
for this the Lord of glory bled,
that all might know 'tis finishèd.

'tis finishèd: the creature owed
a debt he ne'er could pay to God:
our sins had earn'd the wrath of heaven;
that debt is paid, those sins forgiven:
the Son hath suffered in our stead,
and we are freed: 'tis finishèd.

'tis finishèd: remains there aught
for us to finish? idle thought!
He did that work alone, yet He
bestows on all its blessings free,
who with their Lord to sin are dead
and live to God: 'tis finishèd.

'tis finishèd: the mighty Son
o'er death and hell the conquest won;
'for me the anguish,' man may cry,
'for me the shame of Calvary:
for me that precious blood was shed,
and, come what will, 'tis finishèd.'

'tis finishèd: but ne'er forget
thou owest, o my soul, a debt
of faith and love to Him who gave
his life to teach, his death to save:
abide in Him, whose fainting Head
breathed that great word, "'tis finishèd.'

Jesus Christ, and Him crucified.   1 Cor. ii.

ASK ye what great thing I know
that delights and stirs me so?
what the high reward I win,
whose the Name I glory in?
   Jesus Christ the crucified.

what is faith's foundation strong?
what awakes my heart to song?
He who bore my sinful load,
purchased for me peace with God,
   Jesus Christ the crucified.

who is He that makes me wise
to discern where duty lies?
who is He that makes me true
duty, when discern'd, to do?
 Jesus Christ the crucified.

who defeats my fiercest foes?
who consoles my saddest woes?
who revives my fainting heart,
healing all its hidden smart?
 Jesus Christ the crucified.

who is life in life to me?
who the death of death will be?
who will place me on his right
with the countless hosts of light?
 Jesus Christ the crucified.

this is that great thing I know:
this delights and stirs me so:
faith in Him who died to save,
Him who triumphed o'er the grave,
 Jesus Christ the crucified.

He endured the cross. Heb. xii.

WE bless Thee, Jesus Christ our Lord;
for ever be thy name adored:
for Thou, the sinless One, hast died,
that sinners might be justified.

o very Man, and very God,
redeem us with thy precious blood;
from death eternal set us free,
and make us one with God in Thee.

from sin and shame defend us still,
and work in us thy stedfast will,
the cross with patience to sustain
and bravely bear its utmost pain.

in Thee we trust, in Thee alone;
for Thou forsakest not thine own:
to all the meek thy strength is given,
who by thy Cross ascend to heaven.

Let this mind be in you which was also in Christ Jesus.
Phil. ii.

LORD, let the love in us abound,
which in Christ Jesus once was found:
create in us our Saviour's mind,
unselfish, sympathetic, kind.

He in the form of God abode,
yet that bright fellowship of God
He held not with a miser's heart,
but laid his glorious state apart.

He stooped to wear a servant's mien,
and, as a man in fashion seen,
Himself He showed amidst mankind
the pattern of a lowly mind:

obedient to his Father's will,
He meekly bore all human ill,
a life in sad privation past,
and death, that death the cross, at last.

for this by God exalted high,
He reigns with power beyond the sky;
for this the Father bids Him claim
a Name surpassing every name,

that at the Name of Jesus now
all knees in heaven and earth should bow,
all tongues in God the Father bless
the Christ, the Lord of righteousness.

In my flesh shall I see God. Job xix.

I KNOW that my Redeemer lives,
  in this my faith is fast;
and whatsoe'er against Him strives
  will surely fall at last.
He lives, the mighty One, I know,
whose arm o'ercomes the strongest foe,
  who death and hell has vanquished.

He lives, He lives; though dust shall lie
  upon my mouldering head,
yet He will call me, by and by,
  to quit my earthy bed;
and I shall waken at his voice,
rise re-embodied, and rejoice
  to look on my Redeemer.

His promise, who hath ne'er deceived,
  in life and death I trust;
the Lord in whom I have believed
  will raise my sleeping dust:
in this my very flesh that dies
I shall revive, and with these eyes
  shall see the God who made me.

myself shall see Him in my flesh,
  with all his glory bright;
his presence shall my heart refresh,
  and fill my soul with light.

myself shall ever on Him gaze,
myself shall ever sound his praise,
myself, and not another.
rise then, my soul, e'en now, and live
in hope's divine abode:
let earth and hell united strive
to tear thee from thy God:
the bier, the coffin let them show,
the grave, the gloom, the worm:—'I know
that my Redeemer liveth.'

Our Lord Jesus, that great Shepherd of the sheep.
Heb. xiii.

ONE alone hath power to give
  strength upon our earthly way:
One alone can bid us live
  in the light of endless day;
He who, worlds and hearts o'erseeing,
all we do and bear decreeing,
speeds us on our heavenward road,—
Christ our Saviour, Christ our God.
Christ alone, his people's hope,
  vanquisher of death and sin,
lends them power with foes to cope,
  foes without them and within.
Christ, the shepherd of the weary,
through this life-waste dim and dreary
guides his own with gentle hand
to their long-lost Fatherland.
they, the sheep He tends so well,
  drink the fountains of his love,
trusting evermore to dwell
  in his peace and joy above.

if his blessing here is sweetness,
what will be the rich completeness,
when in never-ending bliss
He is theirs, and they are his?

soldiers, for your Captain fight;
   servants, work your Master's will:
fear not evil's hostile might,
   He who conquered, conquers still.
forth to every heathen nation
bear his banner of salvation;
spread his name, his truth abroad—
Christ your Saviour, Christ your God.

        .

Behold, his reward is with Him. Isai. xl.

SOON will the heavenly Bridegroom come;
   ye wedding-guests, draw near,
and slumber not in sin when He,
   the Son of God, is here.
with lamps alight and oil in store
   let every guest advance,
nor shrink ashamed in trembling awe
   from his bright countenance.

come, let us haste to meet our Lord,
   and hail Him with delight,
who saved us by his precious blood
   and sorrows infinite:
beside Him all the Patriarchs old
   and holy Prophets stand,
the glorious Apostolic choir,
   the noble Martyr-band.

as brethren dear they welcome us,
  and lead us to the throne,
where angels bow their veilèd heads
  before the Three in One,
where we, with all the saints of Christ,
  a white-robed multitude,
shall praise the ascended Lord, who deigns
  to wear our flesh and blood.

his gracious hand will ope for us
  the gates of Paradise,
and spread the glories of his heaven
  before our dazzled eyes:
our lot will be for aye to share
  his reign of peace above,
and drink with unexhausted joy
  the river of his love.

The earnest of the Spirit. 2 Cor. v.

WE pray not, Lord, for worldly good;
  thy Spirit we desire,
whom Thou hast promised to thy Church
  to be its Sanctifier.
the light of truth, the peace of God,
  our happy portion be,
the wisdom that inspires the heart
  with holy trust in Thee.
to love Thee, Lord, is blessedness,
  and in thy faith to live
brings sweet repose and truer joy
  than aught the world can give.
o Christ,—through thine atoning blood
  to feel our sins forgiven,

to call ourselves the sons of God,
  and ransomed heirs of heaven;
to know, while we are pilgrims here,
  our Father reigns on high,
whose love protects us while we live,
  and cheers us when we die,
then frees us from our earthly toil
  to share his endless rest,
and sing with angels round his throne
  the anthem of the blest:—
these are thy Spirit's gifts: o send
  that Spirit from above,
to bless us on our heavenward path
  with faith and hope and love.

Renewing of the Holy Ghost. Tit. iii.

WHEN, o Saviour, shall we be
perfectly renewed in Thee,
poor and vile in our own eyes,
only in thy wisdom wise;
only Thee content to know,
dead to other things below;
only guided by thy light,
only mighty in thy might?

so may we thy Spirit know:
as He listeth let Him blow;
hidden let his pathway be,
so He make us one with Thee;
so He bid our lives express
all thy heights of holiness;
and our souls as sweetly prove
all thy depths of humble love.

God over all, blessed for ever. Rom. ix.

ETERNAL Source of life and light,
all-wise, all-ruling, infinite,
Thee, Father, Son, and Spirit, Thee
we worship, holy Trinity.

ere yet creation peopled space,
ere time began its measured race,
thy uncreated glory shone,
mysterious Essence, Three in One.

the angel hosts were made by Thee,
the heavens and earth by thy decree:
thy conquering might on rebels trod,
and hell receives the foes of God.

the Son to nature's formless night
spake God's strong word, and there was light:
the Spirit moved upon the deep,
and worlds their ordered courses keep.

for man thy creature, sinful man,
thy love decreed salvation's plan:
the Father gave the Son to die,
the Holy Ghost to sanctify.

when Christ incarnate deigned to lave
his spotless flesh in Jordan's wave,
the Spirit, as a dove, was shown,
the Father's voice approved his Son.

o Father, Son, and Holy Ghost,
thy heralds speed from coast to coast,
all nations telling of thy fame,
baptizing in thy glorious Name.

Christ Jesu's grace, the love of God,
a heart the Spirit's pure abode,
such blessing holy Paul implored:
vouchsafe to us that blessing, Lord.

TRANSLATED AND ORIGINAL.

o Son of God, o Son of man,
whose love removed the Father's ban,
the Spirit send, that love to crown,
and seal us evermore thine own.

eternal Source of life and light,
all-wise, all-ruling, infinite,
Thee, Father, Son, and Spirit, Thee
we worship, holy Trinity.

Who is like unto the Lord our God? Ps. cxiii.

O YE who on his service wait,
praise ye the Lord, for He is great:
　　praise to his Name be given:
from this time forth for evermore,
from east to west his Name adore,
　　the Lord of earth and heaven.

above all nations rules on high
our God; beyond the starry sky
　　his glory far extendeth:
whom with the Lord will ye compare?
seated in highest heaven, his care
　　to earthly scenes descendeth.

He hears the needy when they cry:
He lifts the poor from misery
　　to sit in princely places:
to all who want his mercies come,
and oft He fills the childless home
　　with children's pleasant faces.

ye desolate, his aid implore:
ye saints of God, his grace adore:
　　praise to his Name be given:
let earth, let heaven's angelic host
praise Father, Son, and Holy Ghost,
　　the God of earth and heaven.

His work is worthy to be praised. Ps. cxi.

PRAISE the Lord: with exultation
  shall my heart his praise proclaim,
in the holy congregation
  sing thanksgivings to his Name.
great are all his works, and sought
  by the saints who love his glory,
musing in their secret thought
  how to spread the wondrous story.

God is good: to them that fear Him ·
  tender mercy showing still;
all the righteous, who revere Him,
  feeding with a constant will.
to his saints redemption came,
  as his faithful word had spoken;
holy and revered his Name,
  and his covenant stands unbroken.

in the fear of God is grounded
  all the wisdom of the wise:
on this rock securely founded
  faith believes and hope relies.
Holy Father, praise be thine;
  praise, O Son, for thy salvation:
Holy Spirit, Light divine,
  sanctify our adoration.

Do all in the name of the Lord Jesus. Col. iii.

HAIL, thou glorious, thou victorious
  heart-enlivening Christmas morn!
angels are singing, heaven is ringing,
  'earth be glad, for the Christ is born.'

hail, thou glorious, thou victorious
  heart-enlivening Easter morn!
Grave, from thy prison Jesus hath risen,
  tyrant Death of his sting is shorn.

hail, thou glorious, thou victorious
  heart-enlivening Whitsun morn!
Spirit, be near us, strengthen and cheer us,
  leave, o leave not the Church forlorn.

hail, thou glorious, thou victorious
  heart-enlivening Sunday morn!
from toil and sadness rising to gladness,
  Christians, bless we the Sabbath dawn.

hail, thou glorious, thou victorious
  heart-awakening Judgment morn!
Lamb of God, wake us, to thy joy take us;
  let our names on thy breast be borne.

The Light shineth in darkness. John i.

DAYSPRING of eternity,
  light of uncreated light,
let us all this morning see
  thy pure effluence, full and bright,
scattering with its holy ray
    night away.

to our thirsting souls impart
  thy sweet matin-dews of love,
breathing into every heart
  gentlest influence from above;
and with grace our lives defend
    to the end.

shrivel in thy fervid blaze
  our cold works of unconcern;
that with morn's reviving rays
  our enkindled hearts may burn,
and, ere death and doom shall be,
  live to Thee.

orient splendour of the skies,
  grant that on the judgment morn
from the dust our flesh may rise,
  and, to nobler being born,
in a higher happier place
  run its race.

through these dim and dangerous years
  guide us with thy lamp of love;
lead us from this vale of tears
  to thy peaceful realm above,
where in light our souls shall rest
  ever blest.

Thou, Lord, only makest me dwell in safety. Ps. iv.

FOR life and light and wants supplied
I thank my God at eventide.
Father of mercies, lend thine ear;
o shed upon my parents dear
thy choicest blessings from above,
and make me worthy of their love.
on all my friends bestow thy grace,
on all who want, on all our race.
the Church and those who teach therein,
direct and strengthen, souls to win;
and Queen and people ever bless
with health and peace and holiness.

may thy good Spirit condescend
to be my comforter and friend:
and still, o Lord, to me impart
a contrite, pure, and loving heart,
that I may lay me down to rest
by Thee protected, pardoned, blest;
that after my last sleep I may
awake to thine eternal day,
through Jesus Christ, who died to save,
and rose to glory from the grave,
that sinful men might be forgiven,
and reign with Him redeemed in heaven.
                                    Amen.

Mine eyes prevent the night watches. Ps. cxix.

LORD, in whom I live and move,
to thy ever-present love
I commend my weary head:
let thine angels guard my bed;
save me from ensnaring foes:
seal my eyes in sweet repose:
in the morning let me rise
stronger, better, and more wise.
thanks and praise and glory be,
Father, Spirit, Son, to Thee. Amen.

As it began to dawn toward the first day of the week.
Matt. xxviii.

ANOTHER week is past, and I
am nearer to eternity.
with contrite spirit I confess,
o God, my daily sinfulness,

forgotten duties, wavering will,
unhallowed acts, and thoughts of ill.
in the dear Name of Him who died
for guilty sinners crucified,
Father, thine erring child forgive,
and to thy glory let me live.
prepare my soul, o God, I pray,
to profit by thy sacred day;
calm may I rest and cheerful rise
to seek thy courts with sacrifice.
      Amen.

The law of the Lord is an undefiled law, converting the soul. Ps. xix.

SWEET is thy soul-restoring word,
 thy law which makes the simple wise;
heart-soothing are thy statutes, Lord;
 thy truth is light unto the eyes;
thy fear abides for ever pure,
thy judgments, true and right, endure.

more precious to the soul they are
 than gold that from the furnace gleams;
than honey's sweetness sweeter far,
 when newly from the comb it streams.
they duly warn thy servant, Lord;
in keeping them is rich reward.

his errors who can understand?
 o cleanse me from my secret sin:
from daring guilt restrain my hand,
 nor let presumption reign within,
that, harmless from the great offence,
my feet may walk in innocence.

o grant that every spoken word,
  and every thought that stirs my mind,
may reach thy mercy-seat, o Lord,
  and in thy sight acceptance find,
o Rock of strength, on whom I rest,
o my Redeemer, ever blest.

Serve the Lord with gladness, and come before his presence with a song. Ps. c.

Sing unto the Lord with mirth,
all ye nations of the earth:
serve the Lord with holy glee,
shout before Him joyfully.

know, the Lord is God alone;
his hand made us, not our own;
we, the people of his love,
sheep that in his pasture rove.

in his gates thanksgiving raise,
come into his courts with praise;
own his kindness, tell his fame;
laud and bless his glorious Name.

bless the Lord: for good is He,
merciful eternally;
and his faithfulness secure
shall from age to age endure.

APPENDIX II.

(1).   SERMON III. p. 33. ("Childhood.")

'He was constantly to be seen in the many rich art-galleries of Dresden. Raphael's divine Madonna di San Sisto was his especial favourite; he has written some lines on it that wonderfully characterize the strange, startled, rapt expression in the eye of the child Jesus.

Sie trägt zur Welt ihn, und er schaut entsetzt
In ihrer Gräu'l chaotische Verwirrung,
In ihres Tobens wilde Raserei,
In ihres Treibens nie geheilte Thorheit,
In ihrer Qualen nie gestillten Schmerz;
Entsetzt: doch strahlet Ruh' und Zuversicht
Und Siegesglanz sein Aug', verkündigend
Schon der Erlösung ewige Gewissheit.'

Schopenhauer's Life and Philosophy,
by HELEN ZIMMERN.

The foregoing lines may be (inadequately) rendered:

She brings him to the world, and shuddering He
Looks on its blind chaotic wickedness,
The wild infuriation of its rage,
The never-changing folly of its course,
The never-slumbering anguish of its pains:—

Shuddering—yet repose and confidence
And triumph beaming from his eye proclaim
Already the eternally decreed
Assurance of Redemption.

In the same volume (p. 124) occurs the following passage:

"The Catholic religion is an order to obtain heaven by begging, because it would be too troublesome to earn it.'

By 'the Catholic' Schopenhauer meant 'the Roman Catholic' religion. But his caustic remark deserves the careful consideration of many who are not within the pale of the Roman Church.

(2). SERMON VII. p. 102, l. 1.

("Christianity glorifies the rags of Lazarus.")

This, I must own, is too rhetorically stated: but, interpreted by what is said before (1.), it ought not to be misunderstood. The glory does not lie in the rags, but in the faith, hope, and love of the heart beneath them, and in the future reward of these:—all which the parable indirectly cited implies.

(3). After preaching in December, 1853, the Sermon marked VIII. in this volume, the preacher, being invited by the Mayor of Bath at a public dinner to propose 'The pious Memory of King Edward VI.,' obeyed in the following words:

'Although from this enlightened company, or from the Masters of King Edward's Schools, many better representatives of this toast might have been found, there are none perhaps who owe a deeper debt of gratitude to Edward's memory than myself, connected as I have been from my birth to the present hour, as boy and man, scholar and master, with the foundations of that saintly prince. If, Sir, a pious and wise sovereign were a gift capable of being perpetually secured to every generation of subjects, I might be as firm an absolutist as Hobbes or Filmer, as Polignac or Metternich. I quite agree with the old poet that true liberty, good as it is always, is nowhere better than under a pious king; and therefore we must deeply regret that in the firmament of history pious kings emerge too few and far between, 'fair as a star when only one is shining in the sky.' Among such stars we justly place our royal benefactor, the Sixth Edward. After the admirable portraiture of this good prince, drawn by your head-master in the Town Hall this morning, it would be a work of supererogation in the worst taste, were I to follow in the same track; it would be an attempt to gild refined gold and paint the lily. I will therefore only say that the enlightened love of learning, above all of the godly learning then justly described, impelled Edward, by God's grace, to rescue from the harpies of courtly corruption the yet unappropriated spoils of a pillaged Church, and to devote them to the sacred uses of education. We are not entitled to lament the short term of Edward's earthly career: for if that alone is true life which we live well, the youth who in three short years had founded thirty seats of learning, had in those years lived a long life of eminent usefulness. This name of Edward is associated in English annals with scenes of guilt and anguish, as well as of virtue and renown. From such scenes our royal benefactor stood far aloof. If happier in his life and death than the princes whose fate has left a dark stain of blood upon the castles of Corfe and Berkeley, upon the field of Tewkesbury, and the Tower of London, we also deem him happier than the mighty victors and mighty lords whose knightly prowess and warlike skill are blazoned in the scrolls of fame. Two centuries before him, another princely Edward, in youthful bloom, the flower of chivalry and pink of courtesy, bore England's banner to victory in the plains of Picardy and Poitou; but neither Crecy red nor fell Poitiers, brilliant as they are with all the pomp and circumstance of glorious war, deserve so well the grateful memory of the good as the scholastic foundations of our Edward. The blood that was shed in those fatal fields of glory sank beneath the earth, and bore no harvest of abiding usefulness. The ink that wrote these charters has been an ever welling fount of learning and piety to countless generations of our countrymen. Therefore we say, with all our heart—*Cedant arma togæ, concedat laurea laudi*. But, while we give so much to memory, let us give something to hope. Let us remember that we possess a living Edward, the expectancy and rose of the fair state—Albert Edward, Prince of Wales—a boy rich in hopeful promise, and having every advantage which enlightened parents and able tutors can confer upon him. Let us humbly hope that Providence may be pleased to endow him richly with all blessings. Long may it be ere he is called to his ancestral throne. But when that time shall at last come, may he unite the policy of the first and the glory of the third Edward, with the chivalrous and courtly graces of the Black Prince; above all with the learning, the gentleness, the piety, and the public spirit of our benefactor. May he leave a large posterity, like the son of Alfred, but happier far in their character and lives; may he descend to the grave full of years, like the aged Confessor; may the blessings of grateful millions attend him thither; and may future generations of Englishmen unite with their festal commemorations the name of Albert Edward, as I now propose that we recall "The pious memory of Edward the Sixth."¹

CAMBRIDGE: PRINTED BY C. J. CLAY, M.A. AT THE UNIVERSITY PRESS.

www.ingramcontent.com/pod-product-compliance
Lightning Source LLC
Chambersburg PA
CBHW030820230426
43667CB00008B/1302